Getting There
with Grace

D0029210

Getting There
with Grace

Simple Exercises for
Experiencing Joy

Lisa Marie Coffey

JOURNEY EDITIONS
Boston · Tokyo · Singapore

First published in 2001 by Journey Editions, an imprint of Periplus Editions (HK) Ltd, with editorial offices at 153 Milk Street, Boston, Massachusetts 02109.

Library of Congress Cataloging-in-Publication Data

Coffey, Lisa Marie.
Getting there with grace : simple exercises for experiencing joy / Lisa Marie Coffey.–
1st Ed.
p. cm
ISBN 1-58290-031-0
Religious life. I. Title.
BL624 .C64 2001
291.4'41–dc21
2001029304

Distributed by

USA	Japan	Southeast Asia
Tuttle Publishing	Tuttle Shokai Ltd	Berkeley Books Pte Ltd
Distribution Center	1-21-13, Seki	5 Little Road #08-01
Airport Industrial Park	Tama-ku, Kawasaki-shi	Singapore 536983
364 Innovation Drive	Kanagawa-ken 214-0022,	Tel: (65) 280-1330
North Clarendon, VT	Japan	Fax: (65) 280-6290
05759-9436	Tel: (044) 833-0225	
Tel: (802) 773-8930	Fax: (044) 822-0413	
Tel: (800) 526-2778		

First edition
06 05 04 03 02 01 10 9 8 7 6 5 4 3 2 1

Design by Feron Design
Printed in the United States of America

To PC with love

and

To One and All of us with joy!

Table of Contents

Acknowledgments viii
Foreword by David Simon, M.D. ix
Preface x

Week One: *We Can't Be Lost, Because We're Loved* 1
Keyword: LOVE

Week Two: *Different Roads, Same Destination* 17
Keyword: ALL

Week Three: *Your Own Point of View* .31
Keyword: CREATION

Week Four: *The Highest Mountain* 43
Keyword: LIVE

Week Five: *Rest Stops* 55
Keyword: NOW

Week Six: *Left Turn, Right Turn* 71
Keyword: RESPONSIBLY

Week Seven: *By Bus or by Train* 83
Keyword: CONNECT

Week Eight: *Are We There Yet?* 95
Keyword: MIND

Week Nine: *The Welcome Wagon* 107
Keyword: ACTION

Addendum: *The Map* 115
Love All Creation. Live Now Responsibly.
Connect Mind and Action.

Acknowledgments

The road that's led to this book has been an interesting one, indeed! Thank you to all my friends and loved ones who have helped me along the way. We have learned from each other and grown from the experience, and I look forward to sharing more of the journey with all of you.

My heartfelt gratitude goes to Deepak Chopra, David Simon, Roger Gabriel, and everyone at the Chopra Center for Well Being in La Jolla, California. Namaste!

Thank you, also, to the Reverend Sue Rubin and The Westlake Church of Religious Science for your unconditional love and support.

And a big thank you to my "midwife," Caroline Pincus, whose creative energy is a gift to us all. Thank you to Robyn Heisey, Chris Ahearn, and the wonderful people at Journey Editions and Tuttle who give me this amazing opportunity for expression!

And thank you, especially, dear reader, for your mindfulness. One by one, we are getting there and making a difference everywhere we go.

Foreword

by David Simon, M.D.
Medical Director, The Chopra Center for Well Being

Because human beings are not born with an instructional manual included, we are all seeking guidance on the journey to greater well-being, love, and wisdom. The history of life chronicles the lessons and learnings of people seeking a life of meaning and fulfillment since the dawn of humankind. In the great and ancient tradition of Vedic wisdom, there is a concept of a sutra, which has been used as a powerful learning device for millennia. The word *sutra* is related to the English word *suture*, which means stitch. A sutra is a stitch in consciousness–a simple statement that holographically expresses a much broader idea. A sutra is the entry point into deeper wisdom. It appears to be simple on the surface and yet points the way to profound understanding.

Getting There with Grace can be appreciated as a collection of sutras. Through the generous use of beautiful quotations from people of wisdom across time and cultures, along with Lisa's personal insights and stories, *Getting There* enables the reader to focus on one meaningful thought at a time. Whether you are moved to contemplate time, inspiration, enthusiasm, or imagination, this book provides nuggets of truth that can be readily mined. Lisa does not dogmatically tell us the answers to our questions. Rather, she offers the seeds for contemplation that we can nurture within our own awareness.

Use the book as a travel guide for life. It will help you focus on the simple aspects of daily living that can make the difference between an ordinary life and one of magic, mystery, and joy.

Preface

We all seem to know in our hearts that there is some place better than "here," some place where we see things clearly, where we feel centered, calm, in touch with our true selves. But do we know how to get there? And just where is "there?" In the East, "there" would be called "enlight-enment." Other traditions would call it "being awake." In any case, "there" is really a state of mind, a peace of mind. It is actually our most natural state, but because of the pressures and expectations of every-day life, we've become sidetracked. We've lost our way. So we find ourselves on the spiritual path because we want to get back "there."

The good news is we don't need to go to the mountains of Peru or be hit by some mystical thunderbolt to achieve the spiritual growth we so desperately crave. Spiritual growth happens slowly, gradually, in the course of our everyday lives. It occurs right where we are, and it's hap-pening all the time. The journey there is a journey within.

And there's no right way to do it. Every one of us is going take this journey in our own way, in our own time. It's a very personal experi-ence. But sometimes we get stuck and don't know which way to turn. This book is meant to offer some direction. All I ask is that you com-mit nine weeks of your life to focus on spirituality, and I guarantee you will see and feel the results in your life and remain on the spiritual path.

We all know that there is a power greater than ourselves at work in the world. It doesn't matter what we call it—God, Universal Mind, Mother Nature, Buddha—we know it's there. For the purposes of this book, I will call this power "God," though you may substitute whatever name you are comfortable with.

God is life energy. God is love. God is the organizing power of the uni-verse. God is in us and all around us. God is. God loves us. God expresses through us. When we commit to the path, we honor the God within. We are true to ourselves, true to our godliness.

It is the nature of our spirit to grow. When we put our attention on our spiritual growth, it flourishes like a well-tended garden. Our path unfolds before us with perfection. Life is meant to be lived so that can happen. The process of spiritual growth compels us to "figure out" what life is all about. And no one, not a parent or a child or a teacher, can do it for us. We've got to go out and live our own lives *consciously*.

We will eventually get there no matter how we choose to live our lives. It can be awkward and frustrating at times. But when we live consciously, in a state of awareness, we can get there with *grace*. The word *grace* implies a sort of effortlessness, an easiness, a certain amount of dignity. This is when life feels really good, when we're at peace with who we are and where we're going.

As a journalist, I've learned how to find what's important and boil it down to its clearest form. I know how to take information and present it simply and logically so that you get it without having to wade through a bunch of stuff you're not interested in or don't have time for.

As a writer and as an artist, I've experienced "the flow" of creativity and the pure joy it brings. I've learned to express original ideas and to create works that come from my heart.

As a student, and a fellow traveler on the path, I'm interested in everything to do with the process of spiritual growth. I've read the books, heard the tapes, watched the videos. I've taken classes and taught classes. My background is eclectic, and my mind wide open.

As a parent, I guide my children to become the best people they can be. I want to instill in them a sense of self-worth that is unshakable and a sense of reverence for their world that shows in all they do. A lofty ambition? I consider it a realistic goal. We may all live in separate households, but we're working toward the same goal. As our children grow, they'll support and encourage each other, which will foster more of the same.

That's why I wrote this book. Not because I have it all figured out, but because I'm figuring it out as I go along, and I have a lot to share. Being on a path means reaping the rewards along the way, not waiting for the pot of gold at the end of the rainbow. These rewards are in our hearts and in our homes, in our challenges, desires, and accomplishments.

There are nine chapters to *Getting There with Grace*, one chapter for each week. And within each week, there are words to focus on each day. Maintain the pace, and really put your attention on the topic for the day without getting ahead of yourself. You'll be amazed at how many different applications you will find to use these concepts. Write the word on your appointment calendar, put it on a sticky-note in your car, tape it up on the bathroom mirror. Let the word and its myriad meanings and contexts meld into your consciousness and weave into your experiences.

After the first twenty-one days of diligently following the book, you'll find that it's become a welcome habit, and you'll view the world with a new mindfulness. After the first nine weeks, you'll find that your life looks and feels brand-new. Of course, you're welcome to start all over again and experience the book from your new perspective!

There are also many quotes in this book from people, past and present, who, like ourselves, have found themselves on the spiritual path. I invite you to listen to the things they say, because their words can assist in the process of our spiritual growth. When we are aware, life is a richer journey.

We *can* get there from here. And I'll show you how.

Week One

We Can't Be Lost, Because We're Loved

KEYWORD: LOVE

Take away love and our earth is a tomb. –Robert Browning

Everything starts with love, and our spiritual journey is no exception. Love gives life its meaning. It is the tremendous overriding force that stirs the universe. It is a force that can change lives and save lives. It really does make the world go 'round!

We can, one by one, build a peaceful, loving world by starting simply with ourselves. Love radiates. It starts within each of us and touches everyone in our lives, extending to our homes and families, the people with whom we do business, and even the people we just pass on the street.

First, understand that there is only one love. Sure, people tend to categorize love: romantic love, friendship love, brotherly love. But love is love. The term "unconditional love" has been bandied about, but it shouldn't be necessary. It's redundant. Of course true love is unconditional. It comes without expectations or conditions: freely, joyously, plainly. Love feels good; it feels right. It doesn't bring questions or doubts–it just is.

And in today already walks tomorrow. –Samuel Taylor Coleridge

Do you remember the first time someone said to you those "three little words"? We all know what they are: I love you. There's nothing more powerful, or more poetic. Think about that feeling you get when you hear those words. Think about how great it feels to hear that someone "loves" your spaghetti sauce or something else that you made with love. My son Freddy tells me that he likes grilled cheese sandwiches, but he loves the way I make them. Of course, I want to make them for him all the time!

The nature of love is that the more love you give, the more love you have to give. There is an unlimited amount of love in the universe. Don't worry that we're going to run out!

Begin by consciously making the decision to choose love. Then pretty soon you'll begin to live in love. That feeling of "being in love" is what loving is all about. It's a wonderful feeling, and it's ours for the asking. Love is not tied to any person, any child, or any situation. Love simply is. If we want to feel love, we need to express love. And that love can be for anyone or anything. When we feel love, we are feeling our connection with God. So express love, and express it in every moment and opportunity available to you.

The family you come from isn't as important as the family you're going to have. –Ring Lardner

Many of us come from families where expressing love was not a priority. We feel hurt by the experiences of our past and may make decisions based on how we interpret their impact on our lives. The interpretation of it all is the key. We can choose to let the past burden us and repeat mistakes that lead to unhappiness. Or we can choose love. We can choose to learn from the past and create a present and future for ourselves and our families that represent the kind of lives we really want to have. By expressing love we create a more loving environment in which to learn and grow.

The greatest natural resource that any country can have is its children. –Danny Kaye

The law of love could best be understood and learned through little children. –Mahatma Gandhi

We can learn a lot about love from our children. Little children are not very discerning when it comes to choosing friends. Any child who is willing is a potential playmate for another. It's all about love in the form of fun and play. Grandparents understand what good teachers children can be. They watch children play in a very different way than parents do. They've already seen what it is for a child to grow up and find his way in the world. Try to see your children through the eyes of a grand-parent. See how children manifest love.

Love starts with ourselves, then spreads to the families we create. One by one, we can bring peace to the world by bringing the same love that we feel for our children to each other. When we start with love, whole communities are formed–cities, states, and nations with love as the foundation.

There is no fear in love; but perfect love casteth out fear.
–John 4:18

In the absence of love there is fear. This is not a good place to be, for obvious reasons. Here our judgment is severely impaired, and we act irrationally. When we're on the spiritual path, we recognize that we are always given the choice between fear and love. At these crossroads, the best outcomes occur when we choose love. Sometimes this is difficult, but when we look to our hearts, there really is no choice but love.

So, one way to get there is to express love. There are so many ways to do this, and we are given opportunities at all times. There are times when this is easy to do–when holding your newborn child, for exam-ple. Other times are more challenging, like when that now-adolescent child talks back and brings home bad grades. In these more challenging times, it's best to come from that centered place within and deal with the situation appropriately. This doesn't mean coddling or ignoring the behavior, but loving the child and working together to change the behavior.

With two boys, you can easily imagine how often we work on having good manners in my house. Now that they are getting older and under-stand how important it is to make a good impression on their potential girlfriends, the lessons are becoming more relevant to them. The boys understand that I teach them because I love them and want to help them.

Over the next week, I want you to commit to consciously living in love. Each day you will be asked to focus on one aspect of the path of love. It's the first leg of the journey.

SUNDAY: Home

Let us never forget: love begins at home. –Mother Teresa

Home is where we can really let our guard down and be ourselves. Our homes and families give us the greatest opportunities to manifest love, but sometimes we take that love for granted and forget to express love to those who need it from us the most. When we feel loved and can express love in our home environment, it is easier to take that love with us into the rest of the world.

The strength of a nation is derived from the integrity of its homes. –Confucius

Whether or not you have children, it is important to make a home for yourself where you feel loved and safe. Home is a haven, a place to call your own, a retreat from the outside world. Home is where you can feel safe to fail, where you know that you're loved just because of who you are, not because of what you do.

Where we love is home,
Home that our feet may leave, but not our hearts.
–Oliver Wendell Holmes, Sr.

DIRECTIONS FOR SUNDAY
Spend the day at home. Use this day to "nest." Your home is your sanc-tuary. Honor it, love it. Keep it clean and in order. Spend time in each room today. Make sure this space reflects you, with colors and things that you love. Fix things up like you're getting ready for important guests.

Feel the energy in your home. If it's a warm day, open up windows and let fresh air in. If it's a cool day, make a fire in the fireplace or light some candles. Find a special place where you can meditate–and begin the habit of meditating every day. Eat meals made in your own kitchen. Just be at home.

MONDAY: Family

The family is one of nature's masterpieces. –George Santayana

We can't help but grow spiritually when we are a part of a family. There is learning going on continually. We learn about ourselves and we learn about other people. We learn what it means to really be there for another person when the situation is not ideal, which is most of the time. Families can be messy and difficult, but they can also be the most wonderful gift that we're ever given. Our challenges, our struggles, bring us closer together.

The family is the nucleus of civilization.
–Will and Ariel Durant

A family is a group of people who love each other. It can't be defined by genetics. That seems to be where it starts, but then, so many times we find other families where we belong just as much. Politicians talk about "family values," but they're really using the term to mean a con-servative, traditional point of view. The truth is, family–all types of fam-ilies, not just the old-fashioned, mom, dad, two children kind of family–is to be valued. And each family must form its own value system and not have one forced upon it by legislation.

Children can't be a center of life and a reason for being.
They can be a thousand things that are delightful, interesting,
satisfying, but they can't be a well-spring to live from. Or they
shouldn't be. –Doris Lessing

One of the greatest growth experiences we can have in this lifetime is to raise children. Yet one place where many of us stumble on the road to getting there is in parenthood. We think that putting our children first is doing the best we can for them, but that isn't the case at all. Living your life for your child doesn't do either of you any good! We can't sacrifice years of our lives, and our own spiritual growth, and think that this is helping our children. Children are their own people. They are ours to guide and raise until they are grown. We can't help them get there until we know the way ourselves. The best thing that we can do for our children is to love them. Love them and teach them to put God first, in every instance. Then, everything else falls into place.

Whether or not you have children of your own, you are somebody's child. As an adult, you can look back on your own childhood and see your parents as people, separate from their roles as caregivers to children. People have flaws and usually do the best they can in any situation given the tools they have to work with. Besides loving ourselves, the first, best place to practice love is with our families.

Directions for Monday

Today I want you to focus on your family. Each member of a family contributes to the whole. Do your part. Be there. Find out what each family member needs and do what you can to help out. Maybe a parent or grandparent could use a ride to the market or would like some errands run. A child might need help catching up on homework or practicing for basketball tryouts. A spouse would probably appreciate a back rub or a picked-up house. Be especially thoughtful and considerate and loving to your family today.

TUESDAY: Animals

All animals except man know that the ultimate of life is to enjoy it. –Samuel Butler

The word "animal" comes from the Latin *anima*, which means "soul." Animals can teach us so much about how to get there, probably because they are there much of the time! That's why pets are so good to have, especially in a family environment. Animals only know how to live in the moment. They don't brood about the past, and they don't worry about the future.

Animals, especially pets, are also wonderful teachers when it comes to love. They love us with all their hearts, and they aren't afraid to show it. (Well, cats may put on a little show once in a while, but we can see right through it!)

Animals are such agreeable friends–they ask no questions, they pass no criticisms. –George Eliot

Even though we don't speak their language per se, it's pretty easy to understand what our pets are trying to communicate to us. I've always felt a connection with my pets, and the longer we know each other, the stronger it gets.

I knew that Polo, my aging Australian Shepherd-mix, was depressed after the 1994 Northridge Earthquake. He was a sensitive dog, and the earthquake really shook him up! I tried to get him out of his funk, but the message he kept giving me was that he wanted a friend, a friend to keep him company. Of course, he wanted this friend to keep him company in the backyard during the day, to play with him and nap with him. He was telling me that he wanted us to get another dog for him, not necessarily for us.

Now, I loved Polo, so I seriously considered his request. Two dogs would be twice the mess, and I had never even thought about getting another dog before. Most people would think that I was out of my mind, and I was! But I was listening to my heart, which is oftentimes much more intelligent. I figured that I would leave it up to God. If the right dog came along, I'd know it.

One afternoon I took my mother with me to look for a dog at the animal shelter. I didn't even tell my husband or children because, as major animal lovers, they would get their hopes up and want every dog in the place. I wasn't just looking for a dog, I was looking for the dog. We went to the Agoura Animal Shelter first and carefully scoped out each canine. Some dogs looked great, cute, healthy, and had lots going for them. But none of them was the dog I was looking for.

We had time, so we drove up to the Camarillo Animal Shelter a few miles out of our way. The Camarillo Shelter is a much larger facility, and they had so many more dogs to choose from. We walked up and down the rows of cages as each dog tried its best to get picked. My heart went out to all of them, but I hadn't found my dog yet. I was starting to get discouraged and told my mother, "You know, I really want a dog that is just like Sam."

Sam was the favorite of the many family pets my brother and sister and I had growing up. He was an Aussie-mix, medium sized with a black face and brown eyebrows. He was officially my brother's dog, but we all loved him so much. When I was in the fifth grade, he got hit by a car and died in my arms. I'll never forget the deep sadness I felt to lose such a dear friend.

I was thinking about Sam as I turned the corner and looked straight into the eyes of a medium-sized Aussie-mix with a black face and brown eyebrows. The dog was sitting so close to the fence, wagging its tail as if it were just waiting for me to arrive! I couldn't believe my eyes! This was my dog. It wasn't just the way the dog looked, it was an instant connection. It turned out that she was female, and she and her brother were found wandering around loose after the earthquake and no one had claimed them. If no one came in before Wednesday at 10 a.m., they would be released for adoption. This was Saturday. The next day I drove up to Camarillo again, this time with my now very excited husband and two boys. They agreed that there was something special about this sweet little dog.

The dog was created specially for children. He is a god of frolic.
–Henry Ward Beecher

Again, I trusted God to work everything out. I felt that if the dog's owner claimed her, then she would be home where she belonged. And if no one claimed her, I would bring her home for Polo, and for me! I did not want to leave her cute brother there alone, so I convinced a friend to come up with me and take him for her family. We all drove up Wednesday morning and were surprised to find a line of people there who wanted the same dogs. It turned out that the dogs were only six months old, puppies, really. Most of the other dogs in the shelter were older, and people typically, though sadly, want to adopt a younger dog. Our names were put into a shoe box and the desk clerk would draw one of us and declare a "winner."

I wasn't worried at all. I knew that if this was meant to be, it would be. My friend, Maria, put her name in also. "Good luck!" we said to each other as we smiled and held our breath. The first name the clerk drew was mine. I got my dog! I hardly had time to celebrate before the clerk drew for the brother. The next name called was Maria's!

We took the two dogs home and introduced them to Polo. I've never seen that guy happier! Maria's family named their dog "P. J." after a character in a book that her daughter loved. We named our new dog "China" just because I've always liked the name and it seemed to suit her. Polo took on the role of big brother, and he and China would play and nap together every day. They were inseparable.

And I found that it was actually easier for me to have two dogs than just the one because they have each other and are less demanding of my attention. When Polo died a few years later, it was China who was lonely. So we returned to the shelter and came home with Bodhi. I watch the two of them romp outside my office window. It's always love and fun and pure joy with these two!

The greatest pleasure of a dog is that you may make a fool of yourself with him, and not only will he not scold you, but he will make a fool of himself, too. –Samuel Butler

Besides companionship, pets are just fun to be around. They do silly things to amuse themselves, and thus amuse us. Pets bring out the best in us. We can relax and be ourselves around our pets because they have no expectations of us. They simply love us. Besides China and Bodhi, I am "Mom" to three cats, two box turtles, a fat-tailed lizard and two scorpions. There is always some form of fun or entertainment at the Coffey house!

If you don't have a pet, you may want to think about adopting one! Bringing animals into your home brings life and love into your home. Find an animal friend to take care of, and that little friend will take care of you, too.

DIRECTIONS FOR TUESDAY

Spend time with animals today. If you have a pet, this will be easy. Take the dog for a walk or give him a good brushing. Play with your cat the way you did when she was just a kitten. Notice how these creatures so freely and willingly give love. Learn from them. Pet them, hug them, love them.

If you don't have a pet, go to the park and watch other people play with theirs. Try to feel as present as these little creatures, as full of love and energy. Or you could go to the zoo and spend time watching the wide variety of animals that live there. You might want to go bird-watching or visit a tropical fish store. Every animal has a gift to give, so see if you can find it today.

WEDNESDAY: Friendship

Friend: one who knows all about you and loves you just the same. –Elbert Hubbard

Our pets may be our friends, but they are no substitute for human relationship. If you want to get there, you've got to have friends. Friends pick you up when you're down, tell you the truth, and keep you honest.

Be the kind of friend that you would like to have. Real friendship is a two-way street. You can't expect anyone to give away something as valuable as friendship to someone who doesn't reciprocate. One of the best ways to be a true friend is to appreciate the other person's unique qualities. Be the shoulder to cry on when things go wrong, but also be there to celebrate all that's good in your lives, too!

Sometimes, if you're lucky, you'll have great friends in your brothers and sisters. It's been said that you can choose your friends but you can't choose your family. Well, I couldn't have picked a better sister than Marci, who is also my best friend.

Friendship is the best basis for a strong marriage. Lust comes and goes, but love sticks around. If two committed people have a relationship that includes humor and trust, that relationship can last a lifetime.

As our children get older, they become our friends. We start to relate a little differently to them as they become more independent. A child whose parent is also a friend is more likely to open up and talk about problems and concerns.

A friend is a person with whom I may be sincere, before him, I may think aloud. –Ralph Waldo Emerson

My best friends are the friends I've had the longest. Our friendships have stood the test of time. They know me the best, and have seen me at my worst. We've been through more "stuff" together. We can be honest and real with each other.

Friendship is the inexpressible comfort of feeling safe with a person, having neither to weigh thoughts or words. –George Eliot

I met Carolyn when we were both in the sixth grade at different elementary schools. We were at Kim Davis' birthday party and ended up doing a skit about a mechanical Santa Claus. We made each other laugh and that was it, instant friendship. We went all through junior high and high school together. Carolyn was always really smart and took honors classes. I took German because she did. When I directed a school play, I wrote in a part for her. Over the years we learned a lot from each other. We shared adolescent heartache, which is a huge bonding experience in itself!

When Carolyn went off to Northwestern and I left for UCLA, we stayed in touch and saw each other over holiday breaks. She was in my wedding, and I was in hers. Now Carolyn lives in Boston with her husband and two daughters. She's a doctor who specializes in cancer research. I always knew that she would do something special with her life and that she would help people. We don't visit in person as often now, but whenever we're together, the years melt away and I feel like I just saw her yesterday. That's the sign of a really good friend.

Treat your friend as a spectacle. –Ralph Waldo Emerson

DIRECTIONS FOR WEDNESDAY

Friendships, like all relationships, need nurturing. You don't have to wait for a special occasion to show a friend how much you appreciate her presence in your life. Today, recognize a friend's accomplishments and achievements. Do something to contribute to her feeling of well-being.

Make a list of qualities that you appreciate in a friend and be that! Do those things that you would want friends to do for you. Remember birthdays and special occasions. Buy some cards and put them in your appointment book ready to send before the big day. Keep in mind your friend's likes and needs. For example, keep a friend's favorite tea on hand for when she comes to visit.

Remember that everyone you meet is a potential new friend. Introduce yourself to someone new today.

THURSDAY: Attention

Listening, not imitation, is the sincerest form of flattery.
–Joyce Brothers

One way to get there is to pay attention to things that are important to you. Friendships and family relationships–these things are important!

It is a wise father that knows his own child. –William Shakespeare

These days, it's pretty easy to keep in touch with our friends via e-mail. I've got a list of my friends' e-mail addresses and forward them cute jokes that I know they would like. My friend Scott lives in Birmingham, but I "talk" to him over the Internet more than I talk to other people on the phone. He's even sent me photos of his family over the computer!

We know when someone is paying attention to us and when they aren't. The people in our lives know this about us, too. Sometimes paying attention is as simple as listening. Sometimes it's giving thoughtful advice when it is asked for. Paying attention could mean sending a birthday card, or offering a tissue. It's noticing when someone is feeling down. It's being sensitive to a person's feelings.

Life is denied by lack of attention, whether it be by cleaning windows or trying to write a masterpiece.
–Nadia Boulanger

DIRECTIONS FOR THURSDAY
Pay attention to what you're doing and who you're with today. I mean your full, undivided attention. This is a challenge in our busy world, but you can do it. When someone talks to you, listen. Look into the eyes of the person who is talking to you and really pay attention. There's a lot more going on here than just words. How do they look? How do they feel?

Whatever you're doing, put your absolute attention on that task. If you're driving, pay attention to the road, the conditions, the other cars. Keep your mind on driving. Make this experience like the first time you ever drove a car. Feel free knowing that this car can take you anywhere you want to go. If you're washing dishes, feel the temperature of the water, take care to do a good job, be in the moment. So many times we sleepwalk through our days. Pay attention today–to what's going on around you and to yourself. How do you feel?

FRIDAY: Affection

You have to love your children unselfishly. That's hard, but it's the only way. –Barbara Bush

Everyone needs affection, whether we like to admit it or not. Affection can be expressed in many ways. Children respond to touch, and it is important to give hugs. Even when kids get older and they shy away from affection, offer a pat on the back or a handshake–keep that physical connection in whatever way they allow you to. Respect their "space" and, at the same time, let them know that you're there for them.

Gratitude is the memory of the heart. –Jean Baptiste Massieu

The best way to show affection for a friend is to show gratitude. Thank your friend or partner for being a part of your life. When you receive a gift, send a thank-you note.

DIRECTIONS FOR FRIDAY

Make it a point to show affection today. Give family members and close friends hugs. Physical contact (within the boundaries of etiquette) breaks down barriers and brings us closer together. We feel comforted when another human being shows us compassion. Give people at work a handshake or a pat on the back. In ancient times, people shook hands to show an absence of weapons. Now a handshake shows a welcoming, a camaraderie. We all need congratulations, recognition. Offer pats on the back, literally and figuratively, freely. Smile! And certainly, when someone smiles at you, smile back. Show appreciation for a person's good qualities. When you get good service in a restaurant, leave a good tip. Be generous. If a coworker has been especially helpful with a project, point that out to the boss.

Express gratitude. We don't say "thank you" often enough, or loudly enough! The most appropriate way to show gratitude is to put it in writing. Take the extra time to write a thank-you note or to return a favor with a thoughtful gesture. Show affection today for all the good in your life.

SATURDAY: Time

This time, like all times, is a very good one, if we but know what to do with it. –Ralph Waldo Emerson

Time is the most valuable gift we can give someone. We're all so busy and going in so many different directions that when we can actually sit down and focus on someone it truly is special. Time spent with a friend or child is time well spent. Experts talk about quality time, but I think that all time can be quality time. Time spent just hanging out, getting to know each other: These are the times that we all remember.

Some time ago I attended a wedding shower for my friend Marilyn, whom I met while we were both freshmen at UCLA. There were some other women from UCLA there, also, and we began swapping stories. We were all amazed at the silly things that we could remember, even after almost twenty years! We couldn't remember exactly which classes we'd taken, or any of the formulas we learned in statistics. But we could recall the specific way one girl taught us to apply moisturizer or the time a friend sat up all night with one of us nursing a broken heart. Time is precious, so we must use it wisely.

DIRECTIONS FOR SATURDAY

Spend time today with people you care about. Make a timetable and fig-ure out exactly how much time you spend with people you love. Chances are, it's not enough. Find time; make time. Sure, some of your friends live far away and it's difficult to visit in person, but how hard is it to call on the phone? Get out your address book and call someone you haven't spoken with in a while. Let them know you care. Now get out your appointment book and block off some time to have lunches with friends, have people over for a party, see someone's new house. Then keep the appointment. Time spent with people you love is time well spent.

This week we learned that LOVE is where we start, and it's where we want to end up, too. The love that we put into our homes, and that we share with our friends and families and animals, helps to teach us the importance of attention, affection, and time. All along the way, we will use these skills. Now let's see if we can venture out a little further, to some less familiar territory. . . .

Week Two

Different Roads, Same Destination

KEYWORD: ALL

We are all one. What does that mean? One person, one family, one community, one humanity–there is really only one of us. We are all connected to one another on a spiritual level. What one of us does affects all of us in some way.

SUNDAY: More the Same Than Different

After all, there is but one race-humanity. –George Moore

Okay, so we got the love part. I'm sure we've all experienced love for our parents, children, friends, pets, or spouse. But how about love for a stranger? How about love for someone you may never meet on the other side of the planet? How about love for someone who has wronged you? Or how about love for a criminal? Now the challenge becomes greater. If you want to get there, you have to understand that the same light that shines within you shines within each one of us. We are all the same. We may have different backgrounds, incomes, beliefs, priorities, whatever, but we are all equal in our value as human beings.

By virtue of being born to humanity, every human being has a right to the development and fulfillment of his potentialities as a human being. –Ashley Montagu

This may be easier to accept in theory than in practice. There are probably a few people who come to mind with whom you've had a bad experience. Or you can probably think of a few people from the headlines, or even from history, whom you feel are not deserving of love. Or even if you believe that those people are deserving of love in general, you feel you wouldn't be able to give them your love.

The mystic bond of motherhood makes all men one.
–Thomas Carlyle

Let's look at this really objectively. People are people. We're all made up of the same matter physically and we all come from the same place spiritually. When we start to understand this we see that we are not only the same, we are one. We are all a part of the whole.

This is an important concept, one that may take some time to fully grasp. There are events in all of our lives that can help us to do this. For example, I recently met a woman named Lisa through a mutual friend. We both had known this friend since college but had never met each other. Turns out, we were both married the same year. We moved to different areas in the state and had our first children just months apart! We both also had our second children in 1989. As we talked, we were amazed at the similarities in our lives. We both had even taught modeling school, in different places, at the same time. I could just picture different Lisas all over the world having the same experiences.

We are all like fingers on a hand, pebbles on the beach, sisters in a family. Though we have numerous surface differences, we are all connected–each and every one of us–through our hearts and minds and shared experiences. We all started out as babies. We all came from the same place, and we're all going to the same place. It's amazing how much we have in common when you look at it from this point of view. We need to honor each other, learn from one another.

DIRECTIONS FOR SUNDAY
Spend today looking for things you have in common with people you know and with people you don't know. Think about your common interests, likes and dislikes, backgrounds, aspirations and ambitions.

Maybe you live in the same neighborhood, have the same kind of dog, or work in the same industry.

There are many groups that work together toward a common goal, where you can combine your interests by making contributions. The Sierra Club, for example, raises money for environmental concerns and also plans a variety of group outings for members. People who love to knit, crochet, or quilt and enjoy bringing happiness to children might want to join Project Linus, a group that makes blankets and distributes them to children in the hospital. Join a club or group that does things together.

MONDAY: Diversity

People have one thing in common-they are all different.
–Robert Zend

Of course recognizing our essential sameness does not mean that we aren't different. The point is, our differences don't make us better or worse than anyone else. Skin color, eye color, height, weight, aptitudes, interests, what we like to eat, wear, watch on television–we come in every conceivable package. And we should be grateful for our differ-ences. Our diversity is a strength–and one that we should celebrate. What a boring world this would be if we all lived exactly the same!

To get there, we need to follow God's example and love ALL.

There is only one religion though there are a hundred versions of it. –George Bernard Shaw

I have worked for every denomination in the world because one is just as worthy as the other and I can't see any difference in them. I haven't been able to see where one has the monopoly on the right course to heaven. –Will Rogers

Religions are different roads converging on the same point. What does it matter that we take different roads so long as we reach the same goal?" –Mahatma Gandhi

Peace and war begin at home. If we truly want peace in the
world, let us begin by loving one another in our families. If
we want to spread joy, we need for every family to have joy.
–Mother Teresa

Sometimes the challenge of loving despite differences does begin at
home. But what glorious rewards are ours when we accomplish this
goal! In any situation, look at where you can change your thinking to
become more accepting or tolerant. You can never change another person, but you can change how you deal with and relate to that person.

On a trip to India, Freddy and I had the pleasure of touring the Amber
Fort with a guide named Davenda. Having grown up in India and lead-
ing tours for many years, Davenda was well-versed in the history of his
country. We were with a group, and a few of the other tourists were
really grilling Davenda with all kinds of questions. Davenda never got
flustered, but encouraged everyone to ask more. He said, "Please, help
me to learn more!" His attitude, that one learns through teaching, is one
that can serve us all well.

On the surface, it seemed as though Davenda was so different from us.
English was his second language, and he had never been away from
India. The rituals and ceremonies of this beautiful and exotic place were
second nature to him. He had so much to offer us in terms of his knowledge and understanding. I appreciated his patience and generosity.

There is as much difference between us and ourselves
as between us and others. –Michel de Montaigne

The work begins with ourselves. It always comes back to that. We can
change the way we see people and think about them. We can choose
to love not just in spite of our differences, but even because of them.
When we celebrate the differences between us, everyone has a chance
to express love, to express themselves and grow.

It is absolute perfection . . . to know how . . . to get the very most
out of one's own individuality. –Michel de Montaigne

DIRECTIONS FOR MONDAY

Spend some time today looking at how you are different from other people. Don't try to position yourself as better than or worse than, just look at what a wide variety of people we have here. Appreciate our differences and all that each of us has to contribute to the world.

Expand your horizons today and try something different at each meal. I read an article once that said that we each have about twelve different dishes that we eat for dinner and we just rotate them over and over again. Eat out at a restaurant you've never been to before, maybe one that specializes in a kind of food you've never eaten before. Order something you've never tried before. There are a lot of flavors in the world. Dig in!

TUESDAY: Sharing

Since we're all one, then what's mine is yours and what's yours is mine. There's no separation between us or between our "stuff." So there's no point in holding on to or "staking claim" to something that really belongs to all of us. It benefits everyone to share. We've each been on both sides, having shared and having been shared with. It's a simple yet marvelous experience!

DIRECTIONS FOR TUESDAY

Today is your day to share. Remember in grade school when you were assigned to bring in things to share with the class? Think of it like that. Share your knowledge, your ideas, your assets–it's all a part of the universe anyway! Sharing is spreading the wealth. We all have things that we can share with each other. What a rich experience to know that we all bring something important to the table. Be generous with your time. Share laughter and smiles. Bake cookies and bring them to the office to share with everyone. Chocolate chip is an especially positive shared bonding experience!

WEDNESDAY: Partnerships

Marriage is the only adventure open to the timid. –Voltaire

How we relate to the people closest to us is also an integral part of the journey. Choosing the right partners with whom to build a life can be tricky. But it's so important to remember that it is a choice. Some people choose a single lifestyle and that is a valid choice, also.

Marriage, to women as to men, must be a luxury, not a necessity; an incident of life, not all of it. –Susan B. Anthony

A partnership is a mutual agreement. The two of you decide what the relationship will look like and how it will change and grow over the years. If you start with the same basic values and share a common goal for the relationship, it will be much easier for both of you to get there together.

The great secret of marriage is to treat all disasters as incidents and none of the incidents as disasters. –Harold Nicholson

One of the tests we're given on the path is to recognize and appreciate one another's spiritual growth. Recognize and appreciate the spiritual bond between you as partners. I always say, the best choice is to be the kind of partner you would want to have.

There is more difference within the sexes than between them. –Ivy Compton-Burnett

We're spirit first, and spirit has no gender. Neither sex has cornered the market on spiritual growth. When we see past gender to the true spirit within, we develop strong, loving relationships.

You must look into people as well as at them. –Lord Chesterfield

We are–all of us–spirit. One bright, wonderful, glorious, creative spirit expressing as each of us individuals here on earth. Our diversity is a blessing!

DIRECTIONS FOR WEDNESDAY
Honor your partnerships today. Whether you have a spouse or significant other, a business partner or a collaborator, do what you can to strengthen your bond today. Ask questions, such as "What can I do for

you?" and "How can I be more helpful?" Then listen to the answers and act on them!

If you're not in any partnership relationship, look at the people in your life and see who you share common goals and values with. A best friend can certainly be a kind of partner, as can anyone who really resonates with you spiritually. Do something to reinforce the connection there. Call a loved one and arrange to see each other. Take a walk together. Have lunch or tea. Honor the intimate bonds in your life.

The best partners are loving and cooperative, people you can trust implicitly. Be that kind of partner today.

THURSDAY: Acceptance

I say to you, my friends, that in spite of the difficulties and frustrations of the moment, I still have a dream. It's a dream deeply rooted in the American dream. I have a dream that one day, this nation will rise up and live out the true meaning of its creed: "We hold these truths to be self-evident, that all men are created equal." –Martin Luther King Jr.

American civil rights leader Martin Luther King Jr. worked to achieve social, political, and economic equality for all. He was a great believer in non-violent resistance. This great man's voice carries a timeless message from which we can all learn. A life of spirit depends on acceptance of all God's children.

Today I will judge nothing that occurs. –A Course in Miracles

If we want to teach acceptance, we've got to practice acceptance, and that means accepting people for who they are. One place to start is by recognizing the many judgments we make in a day. Judgment is the opposite of acceptance. When we judge a person, or his work, even in the most positive way, we are not teaching acceptance.

If a child lives with approval, he learns to live with himself.
–Dorothy Law Nolte

As parents, we often feel the challenge of non-judgment and acceptance. We have so much influence in our children's lives. I don't think we know just how much and how long that influence lasts. Loving and accepting a child for who he or she is will establish the strong roots your child needs, so that he or she will grow with a strong sense of self-esteem, which will help him or her to achieve success in life. And when we practice acceptance in our households, our children will follow our lead.

In every child who is born, under no matter what circumstances, and of no matter what parents, the potentiality of the human race is born again. –James Agee

We can encourage a child's individuality and self-esteem by showing appreciation for the child's efforts. Children are not "diamonds-in-the-rough" that need to be chipped away at to find the jewel inside. Children are more like pearls that grow from the inside out to be luminous and special. It takes time and cannot be forced. No pearl is perfect, and no two pearls are alike. But each pearl is beautiful. There is beauty in the imperfections, and we wouldn't want to change a thing. When well cared for, pearls become even more beautiful over time. Pearls share their beauty freely with others to make the world a more beautiful place.

*Correction does much, but encouragement does more;
encouragement after censure is like the sun after a shower.*
–Johann Wolfgang von Goethe

As parents, we often feel that it is our job to "straighten out" our children's behavior. But there are a lot of ways to do that. Praising good behaviors can be far more effective than criticizing poor behaviors. Experts say that some children receive as much as seven times more criticism than praise. Shouldn't it be the other way around? Catch your child acting "good" and praise that! Give hugs, recognition, encouragement on a regular basis.

The same concept holds true in any setting–in school, in the workplace, on the playing field. Mentors and coaches know that to get the best performances from the people they're working with, they've got to show support and encouragement: both ways to practice acceptance.

No one can make you feel inferior without your consent.
–Eleanor Roosevelt

Of course, it's not only our acceptance of others that we have to watch out for. We have to be vigilant about others' acceptance of us. Remember: You don't need anyone's approval but your own.

We can't let other people define who we are. People often express their opinions, biases, or judgments, sometimes hurtfully, and we can choose not to be a part of that. We can choose not to buy into a kind of manipulation that just makes us feel bad. Remember your connection with God. Because we are connected to God, an extension of God, an expression of God, we are perfect just the way we are.

If you feel your work or actions are not fully accepted by others, look to your heart and sort out your own feelings about it. Know that your Self is perfect, and that you are perfect just as you are. Then whatever criticism comes your way, you can handle it objectively and not take it personally. Your self-esteem remains intact despite judgment or criticism. It all starts with self-acceptance.

DIRECTIONS FOR THURSDAY
Practice acceptance today. Allow people to be as they are, as they want to be. See God in everything and everyone. Don't try to change things or people; just let them be. Don't try to be in control.

Accept yourself fully today. Love yourself exactly as you are. Accept and understand that you are perfect, exactly as you are.

Accept whatever happens today. Acceptance is also saying "yes." When someone extends an invitation, accept it! When someone offers a compliment, accept it graciously. Accept the fact that life is full of challenges and things don't always go our way, but that, in the end, it will all turn out just fine. Accept God's love, which is available to all of us, every minute of every day.

FRIDAY: Non-Judgment

Judge not, that ye be judged. –Matthew 7:1

One of the major road blocks on the journey there is judgment. In a hundred ways each day, we judge, and what a challenge it is not to. We judge out of fear. That's so important to remember. Choose love instead of fear, choose acceptance instead of judgment. Turn judgment into acceptance by practicing non-judgment.

Nothing is good or bad but by comparison. –Thomas Fuller

If we are ALL a part of God, and we are, then we can't leave anyone or anything out. We can't say that it's all God except for that horrible accident or that awful bad guy or that terrible disease or the person who cuts us off in traffic. That's just our judgment coming into play. We must practice non-judgment in every way.

Judgment is a burden for both the giver and the receiver. It separates us from each other with the illusion that we're better than or worse than. The only reason we act in this hurtful way is to satisfy our insecure egos. But the satisfaction is fleeting and is later often replaced by guilt.

There is nothing either good or bad, but thinking makes it so. –William Shakespeare

Practicing non-judgment doesn't mean looking away. We can help the victims of an accident and work to prevent accidents from occurring in the future. We can pray for someone who we feel feels separate from God and whose behavior does not benefit the whole of society. We can work to rid the body of disease and bring it back to its natural, healthy state.

The best way to handle difficult situations is to be fully present, in the moment, and to let God's wisdom come from within to handle the details. Often what ends up working out in the long run exceeds your limited expectations.

Remember: The only behavior you have any control over is your own. It's best to live as an example, to display behavior that you feel represents the best of who you are.

Many teenagers today are wearing bracelets that say "WWJD" or "What Would Jesus Do?" This serves as a reminder of how important their decisions are and gets them to think twice about things that could impact the rest of their lives. Jesus is a good role model, and he certainly practiced non-judgment.

The connoisseur of painting gives only the bad advice to the painter. For that reason I have given up trying to judge myself.
–Pablo Picasso

As an artist, I understand how difficult it is to separate one's self from one's work. Something I create is like a piece of myself. When someone doesn't like my work it's hard not to take it personally. But truly, we must only allow an internal, spiritual source to be used as a gauge of success. Critics have their own agendas. And they're judging our work, not us. We can choose to take the criticism and learn from it, or ignore it altogether. If we feel good about ourselves, we bring that to our work, and we are successful, no matter what others may think or say.

I've been on the other side of criticism, too! For a while I wrote movie reviews for our local paper. It was fun to do, and I received a lot of attention with my ratings system of "0–5 Raisinettes." But what I found was that by watching the films with a critical eye, it kept me outside of the story. I was much more of an observer than a participant. Now when I watch a movie without judgment, I relax and enjoy and get more out of the experience, good or bad!

Non-judgment goes for ourselves, too. We all know that we're our own worst critics. If we want to get there, we've got to learn not to judge ourselves too harshly.

DIRECTIONS FOR FRIDAY
Practice non-judgment today. Don't compare. Think of it this way: is chocolate "better" than vanilla? Or blue "better" than red? No, they're just different. It takes all colors to make a rainbow. We may have tastes

and preferences, but we couldn't have the rainbow without all of the colors together.

If you come up against another person's judgment of you, don't let it get you down. We can't avoid criticism, but we don't have to let it get to us. Today, choose to learn and grow from the experience of being judged. Remember that everyone's got an opinion and it's just that: an opinion. The Truth is unshakable: God is All there is: we are One with God. Keep that in mind today.

SATURDAY: Respect

A wonderful fact to reflect upon, that every human creature is constituted to be that profound secret and mystery to every other. –Charles Dickens

We may not understand each other, we may not even like each other, but we all share a common humanity, and it's important to remember that bond with respect for one another. We all operate in our own ways, and somehow all of us in the mix make it all work together. Life is profound and mysterious, and we're all experiencing it simultane-ously. Love is like the broth of this mixed vegetable soup we're all a part of. It's in us and all around us and *is* us. Our "separateness" is an illusion; our Oneness is the Truth. Respect for that oneness is a vital aspect of the journey. Today we'll be working on recognizing and hon-oring everyone's individuality as important and valid to the growth of us ALL.

Every individual has a place to fill in the world and is important in some respect whether he chooses to be so or not. –Nathaniel Hawthorne

Respect, of course, begins with ourselves. To get there, we need to rec-ognize our own value to the mix and be true to ourselves. Too often we compare ourselves to others when we should be just being ourselves. We are worthy of respect simply because we are. We can do better, not just because we've seen what someone else can do, but because we know that the best is within each of us.

We've all heard athletes and award-winners thank God in their acceptance speeches. They know that their strengths, their talents, come from within. They respect themselves and their abilities.

And yet, a single night of universal love could save everything.
–Roland Giguere

Coming from a place of self-respect, it's easier to manifest respect for others. Each of us brings our own unique flavor to the soup and the result is simply delicious. We're all here to learn from each other.

DIRECTIONS FOR SATURDAY
Concentrate on having, giving, and showing respect today. First of all, respect yourself. Be true to yourself. Think about what's important to you. What do you love to do? What roles do you play in life? Find your Inner Voice and listen to it.

Take especially good care of yourself today. Eat wholesome food. Take a walk or a bath (or both!). Pay attention to your body and what it needs.

Respect the world, the environment, by doing something positive for your community.

Respect people by listening to them courteously and not encroaching on their space. Respect their opinions and try to see things from their point of view today.

This week we learned that we are ALL in this together. We recognize our similarities and our diversity. We share with each other and form meaningful partnerships. We practice acceptance and non-judgment and show respect for ourselves and others. Now we can take our journey further, and explore how, by doing these things, we are creating our lives.

Week Three

Your Own Point of View

KEYWORD: CREATION

Besides LOVE, another thing that we ALL have in common is our capacity for CREATION. Everything in our world was created in one way or another. So, where was it before it was here? It was a thought, an imagined thing, somewhere in the cosmos. And our intention brought it into form. We have the power to create anything we want to, just as we are now creating a new life for ourselves.

SUNDAY: Creativity

Creative intelligence in its various forms and kinds is what makes man. –James Harvey Robinson

This week, we'll be looking at our marvelous capacity to create. Webster's dictionary defines "create" as "to bring into being." "Creative" is defined as "inventive or imaginative." We are created out of divine intelligence. And we are a part of the divine intelligence that created us. We, in turn, are creative beings. We create–that's what we do.

People are naturally born creative. Every decision we make can be a creative decision. We create our lives every day with the choices we make. Because anything that we can conceive we can create and thus experience, our very thoughts are creative!

*It may be that our role on this planet is not to worship God-but
to create him.* –Arthur C. Clarke

Many people think that they are not creative. But that's not true. We
can't not be creative. It is our nature to create, just as it is our nature to
grow. As part of the great Creator, we can't help but be creative.
Creativity is not just about artistic ability; it's also about problem-
solving, imagining possibilities. Every scientific discovery ever made is
an example of creativity at work. We are given plenty of opportunities
to use our creativity in our lives every day.

*Every child is an artist. The problem is how to remain an artist
once he grows up.* –Pablo Picasso

The way children create is such a wonderful example for us. They role-
play, color outside the lines, aren't aware of any "rules" to follow with
their artwork. One of the reasons Picasso's work is so alive is that he
kept the child-like abandon in his work that first marked him as a child
prodigy. Think about the myriad ways you use your creativity every day.

*To raise new questions, new possibilities, to regard old
problems from a new angle, requires creative imagination.*
–Albert Einstein

Parenting is one of the most creative jobs there is. An excellent example of this comes from a story about Buddha, who was a great teacher
in many ways. One day Buddha came home from work to find that his
house was on fire and his children were inside playing. He called and
called for them to come out, that they were in danger, but the children
were so involved with their games that they did not respond. Finally,
Buddha yelled out something to the effect of, "Hey! Come on out, I've
got some new toys outside!" and the children came happily barreling
out of the house, oblivious to the flames. Buddha saved their lives.
Now that's creative parenting.

*No matter how old you get, if you can keep the desire to be cre-
ative, you're keeping the man child alive.* –John Cassavetes

Our creativity keeps us youthful. When we see creatively we see things through new eyes. We experience things in a whole new way. As we attend to our spiritual growth through creativity, we have glimpses of inspiration and bliss. We find that we are more open to the moment and living in the present. The more we meditate and spend time in silence or with nature, the more we find that our creative state is a natural one. Our creative selves are free to express our spirituality through our work and relationships.

DIRECTIONS FOR SUNDAY
Make something today. Bake a cake, crochet a blanket, build a model boat, design a Web site. Note the steps involved in the process. First there is the idea in your head and then the planning, collecting the materials, taking the necessary steps. Then, voila, now there's something! This can be done with anything, any idea that you start with. You can create a cake or create a new life for yourself. It's all the same process. Use your creativity today.

MONDAY: Imagination

Imagination will often carry us to worlds that never were. But without it, we go nowhere. –Carl Sagan

The only limits to what we can accomplish come from a failure to engage the imagination. Imagination is a limitless inborn capacity. We just have to tap it and off we go. If we can imagine it, we can do it, live it, become it, be it.

Imagination is the eye of the soul. –Joseph Joubert

When you plan a vacation, first you have to imagine where you want to go. You form a mental picture of yourself there and then think up what you want to do there. Then you can go about making the necessary arrangements, setting up a schedule, booking the tickets, etc. Getting there, whether it's Hawaii or Sweden or wherever, is the same process as getting anywhere you want to be, literally or figuratively. It all starts with the imagination.

Imagination is more important than knowledge. –Albert Einstein

But what is imagination? Where does it come from? It's an image, or a picture, that we conjure up in our minds! The more we see and do, the more we can imagine, because we have more points of reference. And the more we imagine the more we can accomplish because we begin to see that there are no limits around us!

Imagination is the highest kite you can fly. –Lauren Bacall

Imagination gives us a great perspective on things. We can dream up all kinds of scenarios and possibilities. We can use our imagination as a tool to get there spiritually, too. The truth is you already ARE there, so picture yourself there. Some Eastern religions say that enlightenment is not something that you achieve, but something you recognize within yourself. Imagine yourself in an enlightened state. What does it feel like? What does it look like? How is your life different? Now make it happen. Take the steps you need to take for that feeling, that landscape of your life, to be your life.

When I am . . . completely myself, entirely alone . . . or during the night when I cannot sleep, it is on such occasions that my ideas flow best and most abundantly. Whence and how these come I know not nor can I force them . . . Nor do I hear in my imagination the parts successively, but I hear them at the same time all together. –Wolfgang Amadeus Mozart

Mozart was another child prodigy, a genius whose creations touch people still and probably always will. He allowed the music of the universe to flow through him. He was able to tap into his imagination and bring it forth because he listened to it. He didn't turn it off or turn away from it; he embraced it. He was sensitive enough to translate the music he heard into notes and chords that we all can hear and enjoy.

We can all tap into the creativity of the universe. Mozart is an example to us that this can be done.

DIRECTIONS FOR MONDAY

Today ask, "What if?" and take it from there. Come up with scenarios for a better world. How can you make it happen? If you had unlimited time and unlimited resources what would you do? Allow your imagination to soar today.

TUESDAY: Originality

Insist on yourself, never imitate. –Ralph Waldo Emerson

Will Rogers is a wonderful example of a creative individual who expressed himself in his own unique way and was loved by millions for it. His life held many challenges. His mother died when Will was very young. He was part Indian and was often taunted by both his Indian and his white classmates for his mixed background. Because of his antics, Will was considered a discipline problem and was kicked out of several schools. He was also the only boy and the youngest in a large family. His father, a community leader and politician, wanted Will to take over the family ranch and possibly follow in his political footsteps, but Will wanted to be an entertainer. Will followed his heart and–based on his popularity with the public and his own writings, which show how happy he was with his life–he obviously did the right thing. He was a true original.

Will Rogers is a great example of someone who brought his inner gifts to the world. What we bring to the canvas of our lives comes from within. We are all originals. We can be inspired by the beauty of God's creation and use it like a mirror. It works both ways.

If (the artist) sees nothing within him, then he should also refrain from painting what he sees before him.
–Caspar David Friedrich

I am somebody. I am me. I like being me. And I need nobody to make me somebody. –Louis L'Amour

Our creativity helps us to know ourselves, to recognize the divine inspiration within. And in knowing ourselves, we become more creative and imaginative. We see the endless possibilities before us. We have more of ourselves to express!

Life is like playing a violin in public and learning the instrument as one goes on. –Samuel Butler

When we get to know ourselves, we discover the world. When we learn about the world, we understand ourselves. Another of life's great wheels.

DIRECTIONS FOR TUESDAY
Each person on this earth is an original, and so are you. You're one of a kind. Find your "signature" in things that you do, your "fingerprints" in your efforts. Appreciate what you can do and give that no one else can today.

WEDNESDAY: Inspiration

I shut my eyes in order to see. –Paul Gauguin

Creative inspiration can come from anywhere, wherever you are. It is available to all of us when we are ready to accept it. Often it's right there in front of our eyes, but we can't see it, or don't recognize it, because we're not paying attention. Our minds are too cluttered with the "stuff" of the day. If we take the time to close our eyes and look within, we'll find what we're looking for.

In every object there is inexhaustible meaning; the eye sees in it what the eye brings means of seeing. –Thomas Carlyle

Each person is a creation and a creator. We have access to divine intelligence and creativity, and it will flow through us as much as we allow it to. Think of a bridge. One person may see a bridge, another may see a glorious feat of architecture, while another sees a more convenient route to travel. That bridge is all those things and more! It's the same way with people. We can't be defined by what we do or how we appear. The bridge is a creation that man made by means of God, divine intelligence, creativity.

A moment's insight is sometimes worth a life's experience.
–Oliver Wendell Holmes, Sr.

We don't have to be Mozart or Gauguin to be inspired to create. Where does inspiration come from? It comes from within, but what stirs it is different for everyone. Maybe it's the ocean, or the mountains, or a museum, or maybe you have a muse. People can be a great source of inspiration for us!

Trust thyself; every heart vibrates to that iron string.
–Ralph Waldo Emerson

When my sons Freddy and Brian were babies, I would drive them around in the car listening to children's music. I thought that if I heard one more rendition of "Old MacDonald" I would scream! I looked all over for upbeat, popular style music that would inspire my kids to love life and be better people. Finding nothing satisfactory, I realized that these two little kids had inspired me! I got busy writing songs for children, to meet the needs of parents like myself, and the seeds of my company were planted.

The beauty of inspiration is that with people, it works both ways. You can be a wonderful inspiration to someone else! We're all living our lives as an example, and by creating a new life for yourself, you just may inspire someone to do the same.

DIRECTIONS FOR WEDNESDAY
Get inspired today! Take a look at what inspires you to create and to work and surround yourself with that.

THURSDAY: Potential

I was always looking outside myself for strength and confidence, but it comes from within. It is there all the time. –Anna Freud

Has anyone ever said that you are not "living up to your potential"? Think about it . . . what is this "potential"? If there are no limits, then we have unlimited potential! Our potential is our power, and we can work with it in creating our lives.

Resolve to be thyself; and know that he,
Who finds himself, loses his misery! –Matthew Arnold

When I was growing up, and even to this day, when I'm nervous about a job interview or something, the advice my mother is always gives me is "Just be yourself." How many times have we all heard those words? I hear them a lot in televised beauty pageants, the confident contestants coaching the up-and-comers. While it sounds so cliché and flip, when you truly know yourself, this is the best advice you could get! It's so profound, really, and yet so simple. The problem is that so many of us don't know who we are. We need to know and understand that we are divine beings to appreciate our potential for growth and change!

Part of the process of getting to know ourselves is following the examples of people whom we admire and respect. But while we can follow the example of their behavior, we must also understand that the path they took to get there is not necessarily the same one that we're on. Everyone has his own way to go. We can't imitate someone else to get there, nor can we ride on another's coattails. We must remain our true, authentic selves and express ourselves in our own way. When we truly "get" who we are, we feel no need to be anyone else or live up to anyone else's standards. Being yourself is the best you can be!

When we know who we are and understand the power that comes with it, we know that all of the strength, confidence, creativity, and intelligence of the world is ours to tap into. It fills us up. We have potential because we are potential.

All our dreams can come true–if we have the courage to
pursue them. –Walt Disney

We create our lives. Everything we have, we have brought into fruition. We are where we are because of the circumstances we created to get here. And we create the path to get there, too, each step of the way.

DIRECTIONS FOR THURSDAY
Investigate your potential today. See how fast you can run, how far you can jump, how high you can climb. Do your best and try to make it even better today. Go that extra mile at work. Challenge yourself and rise to

the occasion. You can do whatever you set your mind to. The truth is that we have unlimited potential. We can do anything that we set our minds to. Surprise yourself by setting and reaching higher standards for yourself today.

FRIDAY: Perception

Change your thoughts and you change your world.
–Norman Vincent Peale

The world is as we perceive it to be. If we think that it is a cold, harsh place then that's what it will be to us. We can change the reality of any given situation by changing our perception of it.

Magic tricks are all based on perception. Can we really believe our eyes? So much is just illusion! Does David Copperfield really make an airplane disappear, or do we just perceive it as being gone? Or was it ever really there?! When the illusion is explained to us, we see it in an entirely different way.

Remember that almost everything is an illusion. The only thing that is truly real is love. When we look at things from that perspective, every-thing changes for us.

All our knowledge had its origin in our perceptions.
–Leonardo da Vinci

All that we know now, at this moment, is because of what we have per-ceived to be true up until now. We're comfortable with this amount of knowledge: that's why we're here. To get there, we've got to be open to a whole lot more. How ready are you to perceive things as they really are?

If the doors of perception were cleansed, everything would appear to man as it is, infinite. –William Blake

There are vast possibilities out there that we can't even see. We are limited only by our perception! We need to open our eyes and open our minds to all that is available to us right here and right now.

By thought I embrace the universal. –Blaise Pascal

We don't have to go anywhere, we don't have to do anything. We just have to be. How simple is that? Evidently, it's quite difficult! We can travel the world looking for ourselves when we could have been looking within all the time.

Nothing can bring you peace but yourself.
–Ralph Waldo Emerson

Know yourself and you know peace. Love yourself and all creation and you'll get there.

DIRECTIONS FOR FRIDAY
Look at things in a different way today. Have perspective. Have an artist's eye. Get out your camera and take photos of an object from different angles. How many ways can you show this object? Close up, wide angle, from the left, the right, etc. Try it; see how many different pictures you can come up with. Find an everyday household object, or something sitting on your desk at work, and make a list of how many different uses you can find for that thing. Use your creativity and make a game out of it. Challenge a friend to do the same thing and see who comes up with the longer list. Compare notes.

SATURDAY:Self-Expression

For all men live by truth, and stand in need of expression. In love, in art, in avarice, in politics, in labor, in games, we study to utter our painful secret. The man is only half himself, the other half is his expression. –Ralph Waldo Emerson

To get there, we've got to express ourselves. Learning to effectively express ourselves is an important part of the process of spiritual growth. Expression is as essential to the spirit as breathing is to the body.

Work is one way that we express ourselves. When we bring creativity to our work, we bring spirituality into the workplace. Our work then becomes a joyful expression. We learn to make a life, and not just a living.

The reward of a thing well done, is to have done it.
–Ralph Waldo Emerson

Each of us is different, and each of our talents are unique, but one thing we all have in common is that our talents need to be expressed in some way. When we express our talents through our work and use these talents to help people, we are using our creativity to its fullest.

When we're doing work we love, and find that we are being creative in that work, we also find a way that we can be of service to others. Feeling useful and productive nourishes the spirit, which in turn allows us to express ourselves through service. It's like a great wheel, generating even more energy for the journey.

The notes I handle no better than many pianists. But the pauses between the notes,-ah, that is where the art resides.
–Arthur Schnabel

I love this quote from Arthur Schnabel because I think that the notes represent our obligations, and the pauses between the notes represent how we spend our free time. The art resides in how we choose to spend the time that truly is ours. We can be creative with the notes and the pauses. We can play our lives like a symphony!

One of my favorite ways to express myself is through music. I love to write songs. When I'm "in the flow," the words and the melody come to me so freely and easily. And it feels terrific when someone enjoys listening to one of my songs! This is another example of how our creativity and self-expression feeds us and the world.

We must become artists in living. To live by inspiration means to sense the divine touch in everything; to enter into the spirit of things to enter into the joy of living. –Ernest Holmes

Other ways we express ourselves are through hobbies and sports. Engaging ourselves with anything we love or love to do fosters spiritual growth. Activities that allow us to express ourselves, to be joyful, to be unaware of the passage of time, give us glimpses of our true, creative selves.

Freddy and Brian's father, John, is a businessman by day. He wears a suit and carries a briefcase and is successful because he loves his work. He brings his creativity into the office every day. Yet in the evening, he's a whole different type of a person. He'll spend hours in the garage putting together one of his model boats. These little boats seem to carry him off to another world where he can de-stress. This is his passion, and another outlet for his creativity.

DIRECTIONS FOR SATURDAY
Explore different ways of expressing yourself today. How do you usually do it? With spoken words? With music? Try something new. Write a poem, song, or letter. Draw a cartoon. Paint a picture. Sculpt. Make up a new recipe. Put yourself into this project and see what you come up with. Whatever you write or make should reflect you in some way.

At the end of this week, we understand that all of life is CREATION. We explored our creativity and stirred our imagination. We appreciate originality and look for inspiration to reach our potential for greatness. We watch our thoughts and how we perceive the world, and we express ourselves as creative beings. Now we can proceed to LIVE our lives from this more conscious perspective.

Week Four

The Highest Mountain

KEYWORD: LIVE

Just as our perception colors the way we look at the world, our attitude affects the way we live in the world. A good attitude goes a long way toward helping us to live a happy life. Others pick up on our attitude and the feelings and emotions that go along with it. A good attitude is contagious and can affect many lives.

SUNDAY: Optimism

I am an optimist. It does not seem too much use being anything else. –Winston Churchill

Research shows that optimists are happier people, live longer and healthier lives, and have stronger relationships. Why not choose to be an optimist? It can certainly be learned. All you have to do is look for the good in any situation. Sounds so easy!

I was first introduced to the concept of optimism when I was in the seventh grade and entered a speech contest sponsored by the local Optimists Club. The topic that the club chose for the speeches was "I'm Just One." I spoke about how one person can make a difference in the world. Besides a trophy, I won a placard with the "Optimists Creed" printed on it. I realized that, even with all the struggles I had experienced in my young life, I was an optimist! It made me feel good to know that this group of adults felt the same way that I did. It made me feel

like the world was a great place to have such good people in it. That little placard has been with me through every move and is prominently
displayed in my home office today. This is what it says:

The Optimists Creed
Promise Yourself

*To be so strong that nothing can disturb your peace of mind. · To talk health,
happiness, and prosperity to every person you meet. · To make all your friends
feel that there is something in them. · To look at the sunny side of everything
and make your optimism come true. · To think only of the best, to work only for
the best, and expect only the best. · To be just as enthusiastic about the success
of others as you are about your own. · To forget the mistakes of the past and
press on to the greater achievements of the future. · To wear a cheerful countenance at all times and give every living creature you meet a smile. · To give so
much time to the improvement of yourself that you have no time to criticize others. · To be too large for worry, too noble for anger, too strong for fear, and too
happy to permit the presence of trouble.*

OPTIMIST INTERNATIONAL ®

*The invariable mark of wisdom is to see the miraculous in the
common.* –Ralph Waldo Emerson

Emerson's quote epitomizes how optimists see the world. They don't
have to impose good in any situation; they see it plainly.

I could see peace instead of this. –A Course in Miracles

The first step in becoming an optimist is recognizing that reality and
your perception of reality are two different things. Reality is that God
is everywhere, in all things at all times. We cannot be separate from
God, nor can anything else. When we understand this, how can we
help but be optimistic? We can choose to see everyone and everything
as an expression of God. We can choose to see peace instead of whatever else our feelings of separateness have us seeing temporarily.
Whenever pessimistic thoughts come, just think again, look again,

choose again. See God, see peace, feel optimistic, be optimistic. What a great feeling!

Looking at the glass as "half-full" is the classic example of the optimistic attitude in action. Another way to choose optimism is to watch the words we use in conversation. Do we call someone "impulsive" or "spontaneous"? While the two words are similar, one has a more positive connotation.

Motherhood is still the biggest gamble in the world. It is the glorious life force. It's huge and scary–it's an act of infinite optimism. –Gilda Radner

To raise an optimistic child, the most important thing you can do is to become an optimist yourself. Choose to see things in a positive light, show a cheerful disposition, a positive attitude, and your child will model your behavior. Once you understand that you have that choice, why would you choose to see anything other than peace?

Faith does not break down opposition to good, it is the embodiment of good. –Ernest Holmes

Optimism is a kind of faith, a trust that everything will work out the way it is supposed to, that every situation or condition is for the greater good. Faith lets us know that ALL things are possible. It's more than a belief, it's a calm knowingness, confident and steady.

DIRECTIONS FOR SUNDAY
See the good in every situation today. Look at that glass as half-full! Train yourself to be optimistic. Make it a habit to look on the bright side. Expect the best and that's what you'll get! Read over the Optimist's Creed again. Smile. Pass it on. Cheer yourself up. Have a good attitude. You can learn to be optimistic. Start today!

MONDAY: Faith

Faith is to believe what you do not yet see; the reward for this faith is to see what you believe. –Saint Augustine

To get there, we've got to have faith. Faith is like the gas in our car. We're not going to get very far without it. And the more we have in our tank, the farther we'll get.

Believe there is a great power silently working all things for good, behave yourself and never mind the rest. –Beatrix Potter

Faith is knowing that we're not alone on this journey, that it's all going to work out. When we believe that God is there in everything we do, we can take more risks, and we can really "go for it."

All great men have felt an invisible Partner, an interior awareness. It is involved in us; we do not walk through this life alone. –Ernest Holmes

We take God wherever we go. We see God in everything we see, everywhere we are. This faith in God helps us get there with grace.

Faith is the greatest power on earth. It is the doorway to realization. –Ernest Holmes

When we have faith, we take things as they come, the good and the bad, and know that, whatever happens, it will all be okay. We're not in charge; we don't feel the need to control; we allow God, Heaven, the Universe to operate the way it is supposed to.

Some things have to be believed to be seen. –Ralph Hodoson

You don't have to wear special glasses to see God. All you have to do is to open your eyes and your mind. Do you see your lawn as this green stuff that needs to be mowed every weekend? Or do you look at your lawn and see that each blade of grass is a living thing, a little miracle with roots and everything? God is demonstrating constantly. We are just too stubborn sometimes to recognize this. But seeing, really seeing, is one of the big steps we can take to get there.

Faith can be acquired or developed. This means that we can put our conviction to practical use. –Ernest Holmes

The wonderful part of this is that the more we have faith, the more faith we have. When we have faith in ourselves, our work and our lives get better and better. It's not just a matter of making up our mind and going for it, although that is a part of it, too. It's listening to our heart and letting God guide us. It's being flexible and going where the road takes us. It's allowing God and the Universe to point the way.

I don't look at what I've lost. I look instead at what I have left.
–Betty Ford

Betty Ford is a woman who could have been bogged down or even destroyed by her troubles, but she chose instead to use her faith to overcome them. That same faith led her to help others find their own faith and put them on the road to recovery. She rose above adversity and created opportunity.

DIRECTIONS FOR MONDAY

Have faith today. Trust in God. All U.S. currency says, "In God We Trust"–use that as a reminder that God is at work in your life. Have faith that your needs are taken care of, in money, in work, in relationships, in all areas of your life. Have faith that everything is going to be okay because everything is okay. In fact, it's perfect!

TUESDAY: Blessings

The lesson that most of us on this voyage never learn, but can never quite forget, is that to win is sometimes to lose.
–John Wooden

Sometimes our greatest burdens end up being our biggest blessings. We learn from our trials and tribulations. We can see these challenges as bumps on the road or as insurmountable obstacles. To get there, we've got to deal with our problems and not just pull over and park. Faith in the best possible outcome for all concerned is always our best choice.

Absolute calm is not the law of the ocean. And it is the same with the ocean of life. –Mahatma Gandhi

When my son Freddy was in kindergarten, his teacher thought he was immature and should be pulled out of the class until the following year when he would be better able to handle the classroom setting. I disagreed with her opinion because I knew that he was very bright and figured that he must just be bored going over material that he already knew. To prove my point to the teacher, I took Freddy to an educational psychologist to have him evaluated. Yes, Freddy was indeed very bright for his age, but I was also told that he had attention deficit hyperactivity disorder, known as ADHD.

This was in 1990, and I had never heard of ADHD so I had no idea what this man was talking about. He explained what it was, what I could do about it, and recommended some books for further information. Little did I know that this was the beginning of a long haul for my family and me.

The best thing that happened was that I found ChADD (Children and Adults with Attention Deficit Disorders), a non-profit organization and support group that helps people with ADD and those who care for them. I was so relieved to meet other parents who were experiencing the same things that we were. It was such an open exchange of ideas and information that I immediately felt welcome. So welcome, in fact, that I spent six years on the board of directors of our local chapter and have served on its professional advisory board.

Finding out about Freddy's ADHD taught me a lot about Freddy and the way he operates, and it also taught me a lot about myself. You see, ADHD is genetic, and after Freddy was diagnosed, we found out that he got this condition from me! Now so much from my childhood made sense to me, and I could understand myself and my own behaviors so much better.

I wanted other people to understand ADHD, too, because so often there are misperceptions that label people with ADHD as difficult, and that's not the case at all. I made a video with the psychologist and our family therapist for ChADD to distribute to schools and teachers. This video has helped so many kids and their families explain what's going on and lets teachers know how they can help in the classroom.

I'm still a big advocate for children with ADHD and I have really enjoyed my work and doing my part in educating the public about this neurobiological condition. I feel that I've been given such a gift with this Freddy of mine. This whole situation has opened my eyes to so many things and people in the world that I never would have had a chance to experience had it not been for him. And I have had the great opportunity to contribute to the cause, which I know has helped me on my way there.

DIRECTIONS FOR TUESDAY

Turn your burdens into blessings today. Everyone has problems to work through. How can you use your experiences to help others in similar situations? Join a support group, contribute to a cause, make a difference. If a change needs to be made, take steps to make that change. Write to your legislators and decision makers in your area. Count your blessings. Count them again.

WEDNESDAY: Possibilities

An idea isn't responsible for the people who believe in it.
–Don Marquis

If we want to make something really superb of this planet, there is nothing whatever that can stop us. –Shepherd Mead

If ye have faith as a grain of mustard-seed, ye shall say unto this mountain, Remove hence to yonder place; and it shall remove. –Hebrews 11:1

It was someone's idea, at some point in time, to put a man on the moon. It took a lot of people working toward that goal to accomplish it, and what a HUGE accomplishment that was! Now, years later, it sounds easy; we've progressed way beyond mere moon travel and have gone to explore other planets. We build on the knowledge that came before us and break new ground for even more achievements that will help others surpass our own accomplishments. You could call it a miracle, but that's just the way it is. It can start with just one person, one idea. Possibilities.

The world is a perennial miracle which the soul worketh.
–Ralph Waldo Emerson

Heaven will direct it. –William Shakespeare

The purpose of life, after all, is to live it, to taste experience to the utmost, to reach out eagerly and without fear for newer and richer experience. –Eleanor Roosevelt

So much joy can be found if we only put ourselves out there to find it. We need to be open to all the opportunities that are presented to us. What fun we can have! Each day, it's like we have this big playground to explore, all kinds of adventures to go on, some scary, some silly, all kinds of ups and downs. We don't always know what's going to happen, but we can sure enjoy the ride.

DIRECTIONS FOR WEDNESDAY
Open up to new possibilities today. Where do you go from here? Make a list of all the possibilities and know that there are many more than you can even dream of!

Look up at the stars tonight. If you can borrow a telescope, use that. There is no better illustration of the vast, unlimited possibilities available to us. You can go beyond, and beyond that, and beyond that! There is no beginning; there is no end. There are just possibilities and more possibilities.

What if money were not an issue . . . what would you do with your time? What are your passions; what gets you excited about life? Anything and everything is possible for us. The idea is to look at all possibilities as just that: POSSIBILITIES, not impossibilities. Use your optimism and let the universe take care of the details!

THURSDAY: Flexibility

When we see all kinds of possibilities in front of us, our tendency might be to pick one and go for that. And although it's good to set goals, it's better for us not to go after those goals with blinders on. New possibilities pop up all the time. We may be diverted one way or the other to something else that grasps our attention. And maybe that something else is something that serves us better in the long run!

In any case, we want to remain flexible. We want to go after our dreams but be open to change our plans as opportunities come along. We can mold and adapt to any curves in the road and slow down and be cautious when it looks like there may be trouble up ahead. By being flexible, we can take detours and see sites we might have missed by sticking to the highway.

DIRECTIONS FOR THURSDAY

Focus on being flexible today. Be willing to adapt. Go with the flow. Don't be too stuck in your own schedule or agenda. Take what comes along and work with it. Remember that change can be good, and good for you! Be like the bamboo, which bends but does not break. Do some stretches this evening, or try some yoga positions–your body can be flexible, too!

FRIDAY: Ideas

Optimism and faith help open us to possibilities. Possibilities are the big picture, flexibility allows us to work within the possibilities, and our ideas are a refinement of them. When our minds are engaged in creation, our ideas are sparked by our imagination.

An idea is often represented in cartoon form as a lightbulb going on above the head. It's like a "click" when all the gathered facts fall into place and turn into something new and wonderful. The light goes on and everything is seen clearly!

It's interesting that, with all the possibilities floating around out there, many of us will come up with the same idea at the same time! Have you ever noticed how often movies come out with similar themes at the same time? Or have you ever had an idea for a great invention, only to find that someone recently already invented it? If you get a great idea, act on it–or someone else surely will!

DIRECTIONS FOR FRIDAY
Generate ideas today. Become an idea factory! Don't focus on the problem, find solutions instead. Ideas are valuable, and even more valuable when they are implemented to make great change. Put on that thinking cap, brainstorm. Then see what you can do about making things happen.

SATURDAY: Enthusiasm

In every real man a child is hidden that wants to play.
–Friedrich Nietzsche

To get there, we've got to embrace life with enthusiasm. We've got to smell the roses and embrace the thorns. Encourage success by encouraging enthusiasm. Love it all and live it now.

Nothing great was ever achieved without enthusiasm.
–Ralph Waldo Emerson

Life doesn't have to be all work and no play. We can learn and have fun and enjoy ourselves while we do it. Children have the right idea–they approach life with enthusiasm and make the most of every day.

Every production of genius must be the production of enthusiasm. –Benjamin Disraeli

When we have enthusiasm for our ideas or our work, other people can't help but notice! Enthusiasm builds when more people get involved. It is a joy to be around those who are enthusiastic, and so much can be achieved.

DIRECTIONS FOR SATURDAY
Show enthusiasm today. Be the first to volunteer. Take on new challenges with a strong resolve. Be the cheerleader for a cause. Help raise money, whatever it takes to help get the word out for a charity group. Encourage people to be their best by supporting their interests and activities. Get excited about life. Enthusiasm is so attractive; be enthusiastic and watch people be drawn to you. Enthusiasm is contagious; feel free to pass it on today!

In the first three weeks, we learned about love and how to love: "Love All Creation." In these three chapters we've talked about how to live with love in our lives. This week, the keyword was LIVE, and we focused on being optimistic and having faith in a Higher Power. We looked at life and its blessings and saw the myriad possibilities presented to us. We were flexible and generated ideas with great enthusiasm. The next step on our journey is to do all this while recognizing the only time there is: NOW.

Week Five

Rest Stops

KEYWORD: NOW

So much of our life is marking the passage of time. We're identified now not only by our names but by our date of birth. We celebrate birthdays and holidays and have various rituals for days of the week. We keep track of time on the calendar and also on the clock. Time has become so much a part of our vernacular that we even use it to measure distance! If you ask how far it is to the next rest stop, the answer might be "just a twenty-minute drive!" But there's really only one answer to "What time is it?" and that is "NOW!"

SUNDAY: Live in the Present

It does not matter at all what anyone has been, only what he is now. –Ernest Holmes

Now is the only time there is. The past is done; it can't be changed. The future can change with a thought. But in this moment in time, we are. Everything, every choice we make, it all happens in a moment.

I am an idealist. I don't know where I'm going but I'm on my way. –Carl Sandburg

One of the most important steps we can take to get there is to live in the present, the now. We can learn from the past, we can work toward the future, but this moment is the only time that really matters.

When we're aware of each moment and living awake in each moment, we will surely get there.

Time is but the stream I go a-fishing in. –Henry David Thoreau

We've all said, "Time flies." And it's true! Time is fleeting. We wear watches, make appointments, run from one obligation to the next, frantically trying not to be late. That's okay because we all have things to do and we want to get a lot accomplished. We get in trouble when we let the clock run our lives. Then, time gets away from us. Our lives become this blur of activity, and we're so busy planning and scheduling that we don't enjoy what we've planned to do.

The past is but the beginning of a beginning. –H.G. Wells

Some people live in the past. They re-live their glory days and talk about the "good old days" every chance they get. While it is nice to occasionally look back and see where we've been and how far we've come, we can't stay in the past. It does us no good to re-hash old arguments or pine over past mistakes or to rest on the laurels of past achievements. The only way to get there is to keep our attention on where we are.

This instant is the only time there is. –A *Course in Miracles*

Okay, we've all had some kind of bad experiences in our lives, either a rough childhood or a failed relationship or an unrealized goal. These experiences often keep us stuck in the past. But we can't let ourselves stay stuck; we have to move forward. We have to work through it as best we can through therapy or whatever works. There are lots of tools we can use to get past these experiences. Then move on. Let it go. Live now, not then.

Let us not burden our remembrances with a heaviness that is gone. –William Shakespeare

One of the keys to getting there lies in forgiveness. Hanging on to grudges, old hurts, only hurts you. It keeps you stuck in the past. Forgive yourself, and forgive others who have hurt you or disappointed you. Little by little, day by day, let go of past resentments and start again. Each day is new; each moment is new–CHOOSE to free yourself. Life will feel so much lighter without all that old "stuff" weighing you down. Forgiveness is a gift that you give yourself.

If anyone counts upon one day ahead or even more, he does not think. For there can be no tomorrow until we have safely passed the day that is with us still. –Sophocles

Other people are "future livers." I used to fall in this category. I was always planning ahead, so much so that I lost track of the present. It took some time to break myself of this habit, but I finally did it. The final straw for me was when we were on a family trip to Disneyland.

I had planned for the trip months in advance and the whole family was looking forward to it. When we got to Disneyland, everyone was having a great time. I think no one was worried about anything because I was doing all the worrying. Every time we got on a ride, I would be thinking about where we were going to go next, which ride, how long the line would be, when and where we would grab lunch, when we would fit in bathroom breaks. Toward the end of the day, I was exhausted. I couldn't even remember where we had been because I hadn't been present for the experience! I was living in the future. From then on, I vowed that I would always enjoy the ride and learn to take things as they come.

My time is today. –George Gershwin

Our moment is now. Decide now to live in the present. Focus on where you are, who you are. Bring that presence of mind to everything you do and watch miracles happen.

Nothing is worth more than this day. –Johann Wolfgang von Goethe

When we are truly centered and living in the present, we can experience God's presence. Imagine how well we would all get along if we could just let go of the grudges of the past and give up trying to control the future for ourselves and those around us.

No day but today. –Jonathan Larson

Take off your watch, put your clocks in a drawer, tape over the time displays on the appliances, including the VCR (even if it's flashing 12:00!). Spend the entire day living in present moment awareness. Eat when you're hungry. Focus on the food and savor each mouthful. Sleep when you're tired. Be mindful of your body and its rhythms. We all have an internal clock that we can go by. Appreciate the time and space that you're in right now.

MONDAY: Revere Nature

Nature is a product of the Consciousness of God and there is a likeness in the invisible for every visible fact. –Ernest Holmes

God is in us and all around us. Being in nature is one of the easiest ways to feel God's presence and hear it and experience it at every moment. Nature reminds us with its beauty. Nature never questions God. It exists with or without our acknowledgment of its grandeur.

The wild places are where we began. When they end, so do we. –David Browner

Just as we cannot separate from God, we cannot separate ourselves from nature. Our health depends on the health of the planet.

When we meditate, pray, or spend time with nature, we're keeping in touch with ourselves. We're checking in with God. Little by little, we learn to be truly present in the moment. That time in silence allows us the space to clarify and define our choices. Nature is important in this process because we are not just with each other, we are with the world and with the universe. The universe is a growing, evolving thing. Nature is a mirror which reflects our growth, our conflicts, and our needs. How we take care of the earth, our environment, and our homes reflects how we take care of ourselves. The condition of the planet reflects our state of consciousness. When looking at the condition of our planet, is it any wonder that many of us feel "messed up"?

In wilderness is the preservation of the world.
–Henry David Thoreau

When we get there as a group, nature will thrive. Our polluted rivers and endangered rainforests and overstocked landfills are a result of our lack of awareness. We need to take care of our planet now. We begin by taking care of ourselves, recognizing the beauty within, and seeing how it reflects in the beauty around us.

Whenever we try to pick out anything in the universe by itself, we find it hitched to everything else in the universe.–John Muir

Naturalist John Muir had some fascinating things to say about nature and spirit. At the age of elven, he and his family emigrated from Scotland to America and settled in Wisconsin. His father was a stern, demanding parent, and John worked long, hard hours on the family farm. He followed his heart when he left home to walk across the country, enjoying and appreciating its natural beauty. John Muir married relatively late in life, at age forty-two. Although he studied and wrote articles until that point, he wrote his first book at age fifty-five.

Muir's legacy lives on in beautiful places like Yosemite. His thoughts about the balance and harmony of life and his love and appreciation for the outdoors touch people all over the world.

In discovering new things and the laws that govern them, we are discovering God. God does not tell us about any of nature's laws, God is these laws. They are not kept from us, they have been here all the time for us to discover and use. –Ernest Holmes

Nature lets us see our connection with the Divine. When we connect with nature, we feel the connection we have with the universe. Time outdoors, in the morning sun, brings a sense of serenity to a harried mind. I love to see grass growing through cracks in the sidewalk. It's a reminder of the warm, living earth beneath the cold, hard surface. The earth gives to us in so many ways! We need to reciprocate by showing our respect and appreciation. We need to take care of the beauty around us and not impose ourselves on every square inch of land. The earth needs time to heal, to be brought back into a state of balance. The time to start is now.

In every walk with Nature one receives far more than he seeks. –John Muir

There are lessons for us in every law of nature. We're a part of all nature but have somehow separated ourselves from it. Some people act as if we're above nature, but we're not. We need to take time to get back to nature, to feel our own "roots," to soak up the sun. There are reminders all around us if we only pay attention. When we see the sea-sons change we understand the promise of spring, and we realize that growth is a part of our own nature.

Let us permit nature to have its way; she understands her busi-ness better than we do. –Michel de Montaigne

DIRECTIONS FOR MONDAY
Spend time with nature today. Find a special place where you can go to feel close to the earth. Make it convenient to get to so that you can go there often and easily. It might be a corner in your backyard, a beach, a park, a lake, wherever you feel nature's beauty. Spend time there with-out talking, books, or electronics. Notice the sights, the smells, the tex-tures, the air. Take it all in and carry it with you when you return to the illusion of the "real" world.

TUESDAY: Cultivate God's Garden

God Almighty first planted a garden. And indeed it is the purest of human pleasures. –Francis Bacon

Cultivating a garden brings such joy. Tending to flowers, or our own herb or vegetable garden, is such a partnership with nature. To share in the bounty, the fruits of our efforts, is so rewarding. It's a reciprocity that translates in every aspect of our lives.

To forget how to dig the earth and tend the soil is to forget ourselves. –Mahatma Gandhi

Gardeners learn patience, care. Getting down in the dirt is a great way to get back to nature. Even if it's just a ceramic pot on a windowsill, plants bring life to an environment.

Each planet, each plant, each butterfly, each moth, each beetle, becomes doubly real to you when you know its name. Lucky indeed are those who from their earliest childhood have heard all these things named. –John Cowper Powys

We can teach our children to enjoy the pleasure of gardening and appreciate nature by doing so ourselves. My sons Freddy and Brian both went through a stage when they were younger when they were obsessed with dinosaurs! They knew every name of every species. Learning about the dinosaurs gave personality to these animals, and the boys found things in each one that they could relate to. They could empathize with the vegetarians (the herbivores) and could respect the "toughness" of the "sharp-teeth" (the carnivores). Stories about the dinosaurs kept these kids mesmerized, and they learned so much.

The "dinosaur stage" fueled their interest in animals. We became members of the Santa Barbara Zoo and continue to spend a lot of time there on the weekends. One Valentine's Day, I got Freddy and Brian each a Mexican Fruit Bat! The zoo has a great "Foster Feeder" program where you can basically adopt one of the zoo animals for the price of their food for the year. Freddy became the "bat expert" in his second grade class and did several reports on the subject. When the elementary school had a fund-raiser to help save the rainforest, Brian brought in the most money because he cares so much about helping the animals that live there that he worked tirelessly, collecting coins for the cause.

No house should be on a hill or on anything. It should be of the hill. Belonging to it. Hill and house should live together each the happier for the other. –Frank Lloyd Wright

Our "space" on this planet should be respected and appreciated. Our homes reflect how we feel about our place in the world. When we're taking care of ourselves and have our lives together, our home looks good and cared for. We don't have to take up a lot of space, we don't even have to own our space, we just need to make the space that we occupy our own. By decorating, choosing colors we like, bringing plants inside, we personalize the area and make our homes a place we feel comfortable. Our gardens, our landscapes, all say something about who we are and how we feel we fit into the environment.

Feng shui is the Chinese system of working with the natural energies in the environment to enhance the space in which we live and work. This age-old tradition in China has recently become popular in the West. There have been lots of books written on the subject, and it is really fascinating to study. I "feng-shuied" my home and office and am so pleased with the results. I can really feel the difference! The system makes a lot of sense and certainly works for me. You may want to look into feng shui for your home or workplace. It's interesting and fun.

DIRECTIONS FOR TUESDAY
Contribute to the earth today. Go for a walk and pick up stray litter. Plant a tree. Arrange some flowers and give them to a friend. Visit the zoo and feed the animals or make a donation. Pick fresh berries and make a pie. Join a local garden club. Do whatever makes you feel your partnership with the planet.

WEDNESDAY: Revel in Beauty, Honor Art

Though we travel the world over to find the beauty, we must carry it with us or we find it not. –Ralph Waldo Emerson

Nature shows us beauty, from the magnificence of a waterfall to the tiny blossom of a tea rose. We can also see beauty in each other and in each of our accomplishments. I find beauty in a wonderfully crafted film or an especially original piece of architecture. All of our works are an expression of ourselves and, when done with love, are a beautiful expression of God.

Earth is crammed with heaven. –Elizabeth Barrett Browning

Everywhere we go are reminders of God's presence. To get there, we must take notice of them. Right here, right now, wherever you are, take notice of something beautiful. At my desk, I marvel at this incredible computer which makes my job of writing so much easier. What a beautiful thing! I notice my son's basketball hoop right outside my window. It's heaven to have my little boy, so active and so loving. An afghan that my mother crocheted for me drapes over my couch. She made it with love, just for me. There is beauty everywhere. You don't have to go anywhere to find it: just look around, just look inside.

Beauty is not caused. It is. –Emily Dickinson

Flowers don't have to work hard to be beautiful; they just are! It's the same way with people. Beauty comes from within. We may make ourselves up, fix our hair, put on fancy clothes, and that's great. But that's all packaging and presentation, and we need to recognize it as such. Inside every "package," whether it's in gold foil or plain brown wrapper or muddied-up burlap, is the same beautiful bright light.

I hope to be remembered as someone who made the earth a little more beautiful. –Justice William O. Douglas

We're here both to bring beauty to the world and to enjoy the beauty all around us. We can contribute beauty to our lives and the lives of others. Our contributions make the earth even more beautiful than it already is!

There are more things in heaven and earth, Horatio, Than are dreamt of in your philosophy. –William Shakespeare

The longer I live the more beautiful life becomes.
–Frank Lloyd Wright

Both William Shakespeare and Frank Lloyd Wright contributed to the beauty of this earth, each in different times, different places, and different ways. Their contributions continue to bring beauty to the world. It's clear that both of these men appreciated the beauty of life and expressed themselves beautifully through their art. They were inspired to create, and now their creations can inspire us.

Life is greater than all art. I would even go further and declare that the man whose life comes nearest to perfection is the greatest

*artist; for what is art without the sire foundation and
framework of a noble life?* –Mahatma Gandhi

Artists have developed their connection with God. They know that the
art does not come from them but through them. The art is God expressing as the artist. I know that, as an artist, I feel a deep connection with
God when I am creating. My work is just one way of expressing myself,
as I am an expression of God.

DIRECTIONS FOR WEDNESDAY
Find beauty wherever you go today. See God in everything, everywhere. Every rock, every bug, every fast-food restaurant, every dis-
carded newspaper . . . it all has a place in the world, a beautiful purpose.
It's all there, and we're all here, together, a part of God.

Pay attention to artwork today. You probably have pieces of art hanging in your home or office that you haven't noticed in a while because
they've been there so long. Rearrange your artwork and come to a new
appreciation of it. Create some art of your own. Paint, sculpt, sketch,
do whatever moves you artistically. Visit an art museum, look at art
books today.

THURSDAY: Make Music, Laugh it Up

*After silence, that which comes nearest to expressing the
inexpressible is music.* –Aldous Huxley

Music can stir our souls. It truly is the international language, because
it needs no translation. Think of all the times that music has been a part
of our celebrations, our rituals: the wedding march, blowing out the
birthday candles, graduation. There are songs that bring us right back
to a time and a place. Whenever I hear "Rock Lobster" by the B-52s,
I'm right back at a fraternity party at UCLA! Music brings out our emotions and carries our memories. It's as if time is imprinted into music
when something significant happens, and we experience it all over
again when we hear that same song. We can use music to remember
our good times and feel those good feelings again. It can be a real mood
lifter!

Music is a higher revelation than all wisdom and philosophy.
–Ludwig van Beethoven

Music can say what words cannot. It's a deep, profound means of communication. It can evoke feelings, calm us down, or hype us up. Studies have shown that learning music helps our brains grow dendrites, which can actually make us smarter!

Music has always been an important part of my life. I started piano lessons when I was just six years old. I stuck with it until I turned sixteen and chose to spend my after-school hours working instead. When I was in the fifth grade, I entered a district-wide songwriting contest and got an honorable mention. Then in junior high school, I took our school play and turned it into a musical by writing original songs that we could sing in it.

Music is feeling, then, not sound. –Wallace Stevens

When I grew up and got my own home, one of the first things I bought was a baby grand piano! That piano is one of my most prized possessions. I use my piano to work out the melodies for the songs that I write today. Mrs. LaFosse was my piano teacher for many years when I was growing up in Palo Alto, California. I would ride my bike to her shop on El Camino Boulevard every Thursday after school for my lessons. I think of Mrs. LaFosse every once in a while and know that she would be pleased that music is still such a big part of my life today.

Humor is a proof of faith. –Charles Schulz

Another way to live in the "now" is to let loose and laugh! On this journey we're on, we often tend to take things so darn seriously. Our practice today is going to be to remember humor. Have you ever been in an intense situation and someone said, "Someday we'll look back on this and laugh"? I'll bet one day you did!

Laughter helps bring people together. It can take away fear and bring things back into perspective. It can help bring us back into the present, which is all there is after all.

DIRECTIONS FOR THURSDAY

Music is the international language, so learn to speak it. Make sure there's music in your life today. Listen to music. Play an instrument. Sing! Try different kinds of music. What makes you feel like dancing? Dance! Let the music carry you away today.

Laugh as often as possible today. Cut out comic strips you like and hang them up on the refrigerator. Send them to friends. Sign up for daily jokes on your e-mail. Look for the humor in any situation. Lighten up! Smile, don't be so serious. Allow others to entertain you with silly stories. Wear a goofy hat or wacky tie today.

FRIDAY: Organize

To everything there is a season, a time to every purpose under the heaven. –Ecclesiastes 3:1

Our lives are so hurried and harried with all of our activities and the demands of our jobs. One of our constant challenges is to keep things in order. Organization is a necessity for our survival! We need to keep our minds, our homes, and our busy schedules in some sort of order.

Some people regard discipline as a chore. For me, it's a kind of order that sets me free to fly. –Julie Andrews

When we realize that there is natural organization, an organizing Intelligence in the universe, our lives become easier. The stars each have their place, the planets stay on track revolving around the sun. The seasons invariably change. As it is in the universe, so it is in our own lives. We go through seasons and changes as a part of our spiritual growth. We plant seeds and must allow them to grow in their own time, on their own schedule, according to God's plan.

Good order is the foundation of all good things. –Edmund Burke

We must acknowledge how the order in the universe has affected our own lives. For example, many families have several members who share the same birthday or who were born on the same day in different months. My grandfather, grandmother, and I were all born on the 25th. My son Brian was born on July 31st, my grandparents' wedding anniversary. My son Freddy was born on November 4th, the same day that years ago, my husband's grandparents found out that their son, Fred, had been killed in Vietnam. We didn't know this when we named Freddy after his great-grandfather and great-uncle. Coincidences? I don't think so. It's all a part of God's intricate tapestry. We're all threads woven together in this beautiful big picture.

A place for everything and everything in its place.
–Samuel Smiles

The Internet is a modern-day example of order and organization. In cyberspace, everything is connected to everything. People who have never met in person can communicate and share information. We can find just about anything we're looking for in this highly integrated, complex system. We just have to know where to go to look!

Understanding that there is organization in the universe should give us some peace of mind that there is a force at work to help things work out the way that they are supposed to. We don't have to control everything in our lives; we can allow things to happen in their own time. Sure, have a plan a, but let God take care of the details. The wisdom of the universe will provide the best possible outcome in any given situation.

Governing a household in justice and reason, through love, is just as great as ruling a kingdom. –Ernest Holmes

One way we can allow for natural organization in our lives is to allow for organization in our minds. When we clear our thoughts through meditation, communing with God, and time with nature, we are more likely to see our paths clearly and make decisions that work out better for ourselves. Our lives are so busy that our minds are often like cluttered cupboards. No organization can take place because there is no room to move things around to some kind of order. When we make that space, things begin to fall into place.

DIRECTIONS FOR FRIDAY

Work on improving your order and organization in your life today. Clean out your briefcase. Organize your drawers, closets, and cupboards. Straighten up your desk. Create a filing system and use it. Update your address book. Update your photo albums. Arrange your bookshelves. Be especially organized today.

SATURDAY: Simplify

Our life is frittered away by detail . . . simplify, simplify.
–Henry David Thoreau

We could all do with less stress. The more we simplify our lives, the less stress we'll have. We don't need so much stuff, first of all. We need each other and time with each other. All the rest is just details!

The closer we are to getting there, the less we want, because we recognize all that we have. We could have nothing, no material possessions, and know that we actually have everything.

To be without some of the things you want is an indispensable part of happiness. –Bertrand Russell

Most of us are in a constant state of striving. When we reach one goal, we set another. After going through this process several times, we realize that happiness does not come from attaining the goal. More often than not, we find that once we are happy and at peace with ourselves, the goal comes to us.

How many things are there that I do not want. –Socrates

We should strive for a more childlike enjoyment of the events of our daily lives. –Ernest Holmes

Many do with opportunities as children do at the seashore; they fill their little hands with sand, and then let the grains fall through, one by one, till all are gone. –T. Jones

Directions for Saturday

Simplify your life today. After you go through your drawers and closets, take all of the stuff that you don't need and give it away to someone who does need it! We all have way too much "stuff" and won't miss it when it's gone. Think of ways that you can make your life simpler today. Maybe you're over-extended and need to say no every once in a while. Maybe you need to hire an assistant. Whatever you need to do, do it today.

Seize the day! Embrace opportunities! Use your good china. Wear your best clothes while they're still in style. Don't wait for tomorrow to be happy. Some people think that when they get a better job, or when they get a raise, or when they get married, or when they win the lottery, then they'll be happy. Some people work themselves to death trying to save for a retirement that they're too exhausted to enjoy when it comes. Don't live in the past or the future. Live now!

When someone asks what time it is, you can answer emphatically, "The time is NOW!" and have a big smile on your face knowing that this is the absolute truth! We have learned to live in the present by revering nature, contributing to the good of the planet, and appreciating the beauty and art all around us. We delight in music and enjoy a good laugh. We recognize the organization of the universe and have simplified our lives to live more fully in the moment. NOW, we are ready to look at the responsibilities that come with being a spiritual citizen.

Week Six

Left Turn, Right Turn

KEYWORD: RESPONSIBLY

Light tomorrow with today. –Elizabeth Barrett Browning

Everything that we do today affects how tomorrow will turn out. All of our actions have consequences. We can live now, but we've got to live now responsibly. Every choice we makes affects our future. Responsibility is response-ability. It's our ability to respond and to see the choices available to us. This week is all about being accountable and living responsibly. We're more than halfway there. Time to get serious!

SUNDAY: Choices

Guess if you can, choose if you dare. –Pierre Corneille

Look at the choices that we make in our lives every day. Are we making our spiritual growth a priority? We need to build in time for ourselves. When we do, everything else falls into place. We're calmer, less stressed. We have more time and energy for our lives.

The strongest principle of growth lies in the human choice.
–George Eliot

Responsibility means that we are capable of making our own decisions. It is also knowing that we must live with the outcome of the decisions we make.

Yes, there are two paths you can go by, but in the long run, there's still time to change the road you're on. –Led Zepplin

There are many times when we come to a fork in the road in our lives, when we must make one choice and forgo another. But that doesn't mean that the other road is closed off to us forever! The spiritual path is not necessarily linear. It has lots of turns and curves and may even double back a time or two. It's perfectly fine to go explore for a little bit and then change your mind and go another way.

I can elect to change all thoughts that hurt. –A *Course in Miracles*

The world is not all black and white, yes and no . . . we all have choices. We control our own lives by the choices we make. We can literally change our lives by changing our minds! So, whenever a hurtful thought comes to mind, change it. Choose to think differently. Look at all the options, open up the possibilities, go through the decision-making process again.

When making big decisions, sometimes it helps to put your thoughts on paper. Weigh the pros and cons of each option and consider the effect the decision will have on other aspects of your life.

This above all: to thine own self be true,
And it must follow as the night the day
Thou canst not then be false to any man. –William Shakespeare

There are opinions everywhere, probably as many opinions as there are people on this planet. We can listen to opinions, but we can only choose for ourselves. We need to listen to that inner voice and be true to ourselves. When we're true and honest with ourselves, then we can be true and honest to the people in our lives as well.

There are only two ways to live your life. One is as though nothing is a miracle. The other is as if everything is.
–Albert Einstein

Everything is a miracle, so there's not much choice here! When we open up our eyes and our hearts and see the beauty of the world, it is so much easier for us to make the right choices for our lives.

The power of decision is my own. –A Course in Miracles

DIRECTIONS FOR SUNDAY
Be aware of all the choices you make today, from the moment you wake up until the moment you fall asleep. Some people believe that you can even choose what you dream about in your sleep! Consciously make those choices today, knowing that it is your decision, knowing that you are basically in the driver's seat as to how your day will go. You choose what time to get up. You choose what to eat for lunch. You also choose how you react to a driver who cuts you off in traffic or to a bounced check that makes you overdrawn. Choose wisely; choose to make decisions from a place of balance and love today.

MONDAY: Balance

Birth and death are not two different states, but they are different aspects of the same state. –Mahatma Gandhi

There is a duality in nature. Birth and death are just one example of this. Love, hate. Right, wrong. Good, bad. Right, left. Conservative, liberal. One cannot exist without the other. We come up against it every day. We can look for compromise and practice tolerance. We can seek balance in our lives. As we come to that place of balance we can see clearly and know that it is ALL God, the extremes and the middle ground. When it all boils down, there is only love. Love embraces it all, welcomes it all. Love is all there is.

Balance is not always like a teeter-totter, where one side is all the way up and the other is on the ground. Sometimes it's 50-50 and other times it's 80-20. It's important to look at the overall balance of things. It may seem uneven for a while, but it will all balance out in the end. Balance is like harmony: some high notes, some low, yet they all blend together beautifully.

DIRECTIONS FOR MONDAY
Strive for balance in your life today. Don't let yourself get off-kilter one way or the other. Be centered. Be calm. Take care of your body by eating balanced meals and exercising moderately. Take care of your mind by not getting stressed out. Take care of your spirit by spending time in meditation or prayer.

TUESDAY: Communication

Prayer is the contemplation of the facts of life from the highest point of view. –Ralph Waldo Emerson

When we have difficult decisions to make, when we're in awkward situations that we don't know how to handle, we can always pray. God's help is always available to us. We can choose to seek counsel. We can take a few moments to go within and ask for the answers we need. We might not get the answers right away, but we will get them. And whatever we end up doing, it will be the right thing to do. The point is to communicate.

Communication is something so simple and difficult that it can never be put into simple words. –T. S. Matthews

Communication can be a problem when we look at our differences rather than our commonalities. Part of our responsibility here is to get along with each other, talk to each other, and help each other out. We need to see our diversity as an asset that actually brings us closer together–and closer to God.

Since we are all one, like we talked about earlier, we can feel free to approach anyone and talk to anyone. We know that with everything we have in common, we're really just talking to ourselves. There's no need to be shy! We're just one big happy family, and we're fellow travelers on the same journey.

You'll never really know what I mean and I'll never know
exactly what you mean. –Mike Nichols

Communication helps us leap over the fences that we often erect around our differences. We all have different experiences that influence our opinions. But we can respect each other's opinions and leave space for compromise and resolution. Listen to what people have to say. We can learn a lot by communicating with each other and expressing our different viewpoints.

It is all right to hold a conversation but you should let go of it
every now and then. –Richard Armour

Often we cling to beliefs about people and their opinions that are years old. All of us change and grow. We wouldn't want our opinions from years ago to come back and haunt us, so why should we hold the past against other people in our lives? It's important to check our beliefs about people against current reality from time to time.

Sometimes people change so much that they're like a whole new person, and they are! Our cells regenerate on a regular basis, so physically this is literally happening all the time. Since mind, body, and spirit are intricately connected, it doesn't take much thought to realize that we're constantly being mentally and spiritually renewed as well.

It is a luxury to be understood. –Ralph Waldo Emerson

Perhaps I'm making it sound too easy. Communication is hard. It's hard enough to understand ourselves; how are we supposed to understand others? By always seeking to understand the person's point of view, even when we don't share it. By accepting the other person as a fellow traveler. We're all on this journey. By communicating, by remaining open to one another, we are responsible for making the world a better place for all of us.

DIRECTIONS FOR TUESDAY
Communication is the word of the day. Watch how you communicate with people today. Are you talking at them or with them? Are you exchanging ideas? Are you listening to what they have to say? Repeat

back what someone says to you today, in your own words, to make sure that you clearly understood them.

And remember: Communication is a two-way street. Make sure that you communicate clearly when you are speaking so that you are understood.

WEDNESDAY: Character

No man knows his true character until he has run out of gas, purchased something on the installment plan, and raised an adolescent. –Mercelene Cox

We may be influenced by people all through our lives, but we are responsible for our own actions and for the choices we make that lead to our actions. It's up to us what to do. At every stage of the journey, we are called upon to show what we're made of, to demonstrate character.

All the world's a stage,
And all the men and women merely players;
They have their exits and their entrances;
And one man in his time plays many parts;
His acts being seven ages. –William Shakespeare

Like acts in a play, our lives go through many changes. We learn and grow and act based on the knowledge we have at that particular point in time. We learn from our experiences and gain wisdom as we go along.

Character is higher than intellect. Thinking is the function.
Living is the functionary. The stream retreats to its source.
A great soul will be strong to live, as well as strong to think.
–Ralph Waldo Emerson

There is a story about Gandhi that illustrates this point. One day Gandhi was approached by a young mother who was worried about her son. It seems her son was eating too much sugar, and she wanted Gandhi to tell the boy to quit, that it was bad for his health to eat too many sweets. Gandhi refused to talk to the boy. Instead, he said, "Come back in two weeks and bring the boy with you." When the woman came back with her son two weeks later, Gandhi advised the boy to give up sugar, that he would feel better and be healthier without it. The boy listened to Gandhi's words carefully and promised to do as the wise man said. Though the mother was grateful, she asked Gandhi why he couldn't have said that same thing two weeks ago. Gandhi gently explained that he could not ask the boy to give up sugar if he hadn't already given up sugar himself.

Some people say that we're often "tested" on this journey. I think it's just all part of the process. These challenges we have to deal with just help us to figure it all out. It sometimes seems like we get over one hurdle and then here comes another one. But getting there is all about seeing that we can really fly above the hurdles, so that there are no obstacles in our way. It's all about figuring out what it's all about, isn't it?

We have not passed that subtle line between childhood and adulthood until we have stopped saying, 'It got lost' and say, 'I lost it.' –Sydney J. Harris

Part of growing spiritually (and just plain growing up!) involves taking responsibility for our own actions and our own decisions. There's a kind of maturity in seeing how our own actions affect the people around us, the planet, and even future generations. Life is a responsibility; take it as part of the package. Concern for our planet and our place as citizens is a character trait that is spiritually beneficial to everyone.

The final forming of a person's character lies in their own hands. –Anne Frank

Directions for Wednesday
Focus on character today. Make a list of the character traits of people you admire. Ask yourself which of these traits you share with them. Look at events in your life which have helped to shape your character. Many times, hardships make us stronger, and that strength is something good that comes of a bad situation.

THURSDAY: Social Responsibility

The secret of happiness is this: Let your interests be as wide as possible, and let your reactions to the things and persons that interest you be as far possible friendly rather than hostile.
–Bertrand Russell

Living spiritually means living responsibly–toward one another, toward all the creatures of the earth, toward the earth itself. A non-profit organization called ECO (Earth Communication Office) lists some things we can do to be responsible citizens of the earth. They say, "Small changes can have a big impact: Choose wisely."

There are so many options these days for being socially responsible: We can recycle, buy organic meats and fruits/vegetables, get involved with community gardens or neighborhood cleanup campaigns, volunteer with a wildlife conservation group, join an anti-gun-violence group, drive a fuel-efficient car, invest in socially responsible mutual funds, use rechargeable batteries–you name it. Frankly, there's no excuse not to act responsibly anymore.

Mother Nature and our communities are calling to us, and it is our responsibility to answer that call. Change may be hard, but it's so worth it. Once you start acting socially responsible , it becomes a wonderful habit. You just get into a good routine and don't even think of it as work anymore. And then, once you see all the benefits that come from the changes you've made, you'll just want to make more.

DIRECTIONS FOR THURSDAY
Be a responsible citizen today. Pick up trash you see lying around. Walk or bike rather than drive somewhere. Donate to charity. Volunteer your time. Visit a nursing home. Be an active contributor to your community today.

FRIDAY: Kindness and Courtesy

A soft answer turneth away wrath. –Proverbs 15:1

Of course acting responsibly doesn't stop with the environment. It extends to how we treat one another as human companions on this earth. It's tempting sometimes to do our own thing–especially if we feel that we're really doing what we love–without considering its impact on others. While we're all out dancing in the universe, the only rule is this: Don't hurt anyone or anything in the process. Kindness and courtesy are the watchwords for today.

Kind words can be short and easy to speak, but their echoes are truly endless. –Mother Teresa

Let's start with the words we use and the way we use them. Words are so powerful and, as we all know, so is how we say them. Kindness can diffuse a volatile situation; empathy can break down barriers and enable us to relate to each other on a soul level. Keep remembering, we are One. Think about how you would want to be treated and treat others like that.

No act of kindness, no matter how small, is ever wasted. –Aesop

Why are we so surprised when a stranger shows us some kindness? Because they don't have to? If we all chose kindness it would surely be a different world.

Kindness can become its own motive. We are made kind by being kind. –Eric Hoffer

It feels good to help other people. Once you start doing so and discover how good it feels, you'll want to do it more and more. There is no better motive for kindness than knowing that it is doing more good for ourselves than it is for the other person. We shouldn't expect to receive anything in return. When we get a smile, or a "thank you," that's frosting on the cake!

Kindness is ever the begetter of kindness. –Sophocles

It's amazing how long the effects of acts of kindness last, and how far they reverberate! It's a marvelous kind of fuel for our journeys.

*Loving kindness is greater than laws; and the charities of life
are more than all ceremonies.* –Talmud

Kindness in words creates confidence. Kindness in thinking creates profoundness. Kindness in giving creates love. –Lao-tzu

*Every time we help someone else we live just that much more
and have started a new spiral in our evolution.* –Ernest Holmes

*Life is not so short but that there is always time enough
for courtesy. Manners are the happy ways of doing things.*
–Ralph Waldo Emerson

Kindness and courtesy go hand in hand. There's a reason why so many people read "Miss Manners." And more classes are taught today about business etiquette. As human beings, we have so many social situations that require us to have manners. This is one thing that differentiates us from other species in the animal kingdom. It's a simple thing to do and makes such a good impression . . . have good manners!

Courtesy should always be given freely and taken graciously.

I can live for two months on a good compliment. –Mark Twain

We feel good about ourselves when we feel that others think us worthy of praise. Compliments don't cost anything to hand out, yet are so very valuable to the recipient. Pay attention to people's efforts and accomplishments and give genuine praise and compliments.

DIRECTIONS FOR FRIDAY
Be kind and courteous today. Use good manners, proper etiquette. Having good manners shows respect for the people you are with. The word "gentleman" brings to mind good manners, someone who is a gentle and kind man. Notice how people respond when you are being genuinely kind to them. It's wonderful!

SATURDAY: Angels

In heaven an angel is nobody in particular.
–George Bernard Shaw

Images of angels are everywhere: coffee mugs, calendars, greeting cards, and garden tools. Little golden angel pins are perched on lapels and shoulders proudly heralding their popularity. There are countless books written about them, a hit TV show, and several big budget movies with the angel theme.

Who can resist these beautiful creatures who represent only goodness and light? I started to think about my own angel collection. I've got an angel candlestick holder that is precious to me because it was a birth-day gift from a good friend. I've got a pin that all of our community group members each received for being such "angels." Although these angel things seem to be all around us like some sort of retail blitz, they serve as a reminder of the real angels in our lives every day.

The mom who stays up all night cutting out colorful shapes for the kindergarten art project is an angel. The friend who drives car pool so you can sleep in when you've got a cold is an angel. The neighbor who feeds your cat while you're away and the mailman who comes to the door with a package on a rainy day are angels. The child who hugs you and warms your heart when you didn't even realize it needed warming is the sweetest angel of all.

The little angels in the stores are just asking us to open our eyes and recognize the angels all around us all the time. Maybe they're also telling us to follow their example and be an angel as well. Their quiet message lifts our spirits and renews our faith. Although angels have always been around us, now we are noticing them more and honoring their presence in our lives.

No one can be happy unless he feels his life is in some way important. –Bertrand Russell

We all need to feel that we are contributing. So, contribute! Help people and you'll know that your life is important. Take the focus off of yourself and your own problems and look at the big picture. We are One. Look at all that you can do to help others, and in turn, help your-self.

Peace begins with a smile. –Mother Teresa

It starts with each one of us. Feel good. Smile. Be kind and courteous. It all helps to make the world a better place. Responsible people smile-it's the right thing to do! And even if you don't feel like smiling, you will when someone smiles back at you.

The heart's earnest and pure desire is always fulfilled. In my own experience, I have often seen this rule being verified. –Mahatma Gandhi

One by one, we can create the world that we want to live in. We can start now, by being responsible people, by caring for ourselves, each other, and our planet.

DIRECTIONS FOR SATURDAY

Be aware of your angels today. Be an angel today! Make a special effort to show appreciation for someone's kindness toward you. Thank peo-ple who are overdue for thanks. Do something special for people who are always helping you. Find what needs to be done today and do it anonymously. Maybe the office kitchen is out of coffee filters, or your church has been making due with tattered old tablecloths. Maybe the kindergarten class just has stubby little crayons to color with. Go out and replace these things and don't say anything about it. Just know you did a good thing! Choose to be an angel! Be a messenger of kindness and peace. Take the responsibility to bring some happiness and joy into the world in whatever way you can.

This week has been all about how we interact with one another and the world we live in. Choices, communication, balance, kindness–every time we speak or act, we have impact on the world around us. Choose wisely, communicate openly, live in balance, be kind always–isn't this the kind of person you wish to be? Now let's move ahead and CONNECT with our true selves.

Week Seven

By Bus or by Train

KEYWORD: CONNECT

We've been out on the road a full six weeks now. Covered a lot of ground: We understand fully the concepts of LOVE ALL CREATION and LIVE NOW RESPONSIBLY. We are well on our way to a new life! We know that we are connected to each other and to nature. Now it's time to appreciate our connection with spirit and discover our true selves.

SUNDAY: Giving

All that I give, I give to myself. –A Course in Miracles

There's no better evidence that we're all connected than giving and receiving. One can't happen without the other. We are always connected, but we feel it more during these times of exchange. Sunday is a great day to focus on giving, on opening ourselves up to the pure joy that comes from extending ourselves out into the world. Just a bit of practice at it and we see that giving and receiving are really the same thing. When we give, we receive joy. Whatever it is that we give, we have more of. When we give love, we get love back. When we give money, more money comes our way. When we give of ourselves, we get to know ourselves better, and that is a true gift.

It was easier to do a friendly thing than it was to stay and be thanked for it. –Louisa May Alcott

Sometimes, I'm convinced, people don't think themselves worthy of a gift. They're more comfortable with giving than receiving. Part of this process involves allowing others to give to us, even if it is just their thanks. When others allow us to give to them, they are giving us a wonderful opportunity. We must allow them to have the same opportunity.

A committed giver is a person who is an incurably happy person, a secure person, a satisfied person, and a prosperous person. –Eric Butterworth

People who give on a regular basis understand that there is unlimited abundance in the universe. The more we give, the more we have to give! We cannot measure the sky, we cannot count the stars or the grains of sand, yet we know there is plenty for all of us to enjoy. The same goes for giving. So much good comes from it, too much to measure!

To give without any reward, or any notice, has a special quality of its own. –Anne Morrow Lindbergh

I like to think of those who give anonymously. What selflessness, what genuine grace. They're not in it for the thanks or the recognition, they just know that their contribution makes a difference. When we give without expectation, just for the sake of giving, we know in our hearts that we've done something good and that is enough reward.

DIRECTIONS FOR SUNDAY
Focus on all that you can give today. Give of yourself, your time, your talents; give money; give things. Give freely, generously and without expectation. Give happily and lovingly. Give love.

MONDAY: Togetherness

God hid the whole world in thy heart. –Ralph Waldo Emerson

We are all in this together! We are one. This is what allows us to feel empathy, to relate to each other, to understand each other's sorrows and joys. The whole world is in each of our hearts.

Man is a social animal. –Seneca

We recognize our togetherness at an early age. Parents organize play groups for their kids, sign them up for sports teams, attend "Mommy and Me" classes. Then there are the scouts groups, church groups, school clubs and activities. We like to congregate together. We've learned that things get accomplished when we work together. And we have fun doing it–together!

We can only keep what we give. Things are made to use, not to keep. –Ernest Holmes

One way to express our connectedness, our togetherness, is to share what we've got. We don't have to be millionnaires to help each other. We all have some stuff stashed away that we're keeping or saving . . . for what? This stuff is useless if it is not being used, so why are we hanging on to it? Give it away. There are so many people in this world who have so little, who would use and appreciate things that are just collecting dust in someone else's home. Give what you have. It might not seem like much to you, but it could be invaluable to someone else. And it will be a great reminder that we're all in this together.

There is a destiny that makes us brothers, none goes his way alone. All that we send into the lives of others comes back into our own. –Edwin Markham

We're all getting there in our own way at our own pace, and we'll all eventually end up at the same place. Recognizing that everything we say and do has an effect on the people in our lives and on ourselves bonds us like sisters and brothers.

DIRECTIONS FOR MONDAY
Find an organization or a charity group that you can be a part of and work with. There is surely some cause that you can feel personally con-nected with that you would like to contribute to. Work together with a group of people and feel the energy of the combined efforts.

TUESDAY: Service

Everybody wants to do something to help, but nobody wants to be first. –Pearl Bailey

Sometimes it takes a lot of people, a lot of work, and a lot of time to get things done around here. But that's okay. Because the experience of working toward a worthy goal is as worthy as the goal itself. So, volunteer, and be the first to volunteer!

Volunteers are angels in disguise! Those who raise their hand and say, "Yes, I will help," are answering God's call. Then again, why wait to be asked? When you see something that needs to be done, do it!

Our deeds determine us, as much as we determine our deeds. –George Eliot

People know us by what we do. We choose which charities we give to, how much we participate in our schools and communities. The people around us may not know us personally, but they are aware of our connection in these areas.

The service we render others is really the rent we pay for our room on the earth. –Sir Wilfred Grenfell

You may say, but shouldn't we be more selfless about service? Sure. But I say, even if we start out doing good deeds to make a good impression, and it's a pretty human thing to do, good work is being done and we'll see how good we feel doing it. We'll end up helping out and making a contribution not to please other people or to have them think well of us, but for our own good, because we know it is the right thing to do.

DIRECTIONS FOR TUESDAY

Find ways that you can be of service today. Help people. Do good deeds. Fix things. Make arrangements to speak at a high school's career day. Sign up to be a mentor. Sign up to serve in some way at your church or synagogue; there are always lots of jobs to do there. Volunteer at a homeless shelter or soup kitchen, deliver meals to shut-ins, donate blood, speak to a Scout troop—there are thousands of ways to serve. Serve willingly and joyfully.

WEDNESDAY: Community

This country will not be a good place for any of us to live in unless we make it a good place for all of us to live in.
—Theodore Roosevelt

What we've been talking about this week so far is how connected we all are. This world is a community on so many levels. In our social structure, politically, environmentally, family-wise. Some people think of spiritual growth only in individual terms. But getting there is all about finding our place in the human community and finding ways to express spirit in the world.

What marvelous results we would be sure to get if we would only put our individual visions all together, synchronize them, and weave them into a collective vision. —Ernest Holmes

We can accomplish so much more when we work together. Even though we all have our individual issues, when we come together we can usually find a common thread, an umbrella under which we can all work. To get there, we've got to expand our vision to see things that we can do to connect with other people. Because their issues are our issues, and we can help.

Never doubt that a small group of thoughtful, committed people can change the world. Indeed it is the only thing that ever has.
—Margaret Mead

I've been involved with several different non-profit groups and it is totally amazing what can be done when people come together with a common goal. Our local ChADD (Children and Adults with Attention Deficit Disorders) chapter started out as basically five moms meeting in someone's living room. Now, about eight years later, we've got over 400 members, a lending library, and monthly lecture meetings with respected professionals. There are also two support groups that meet regularly. The chapter serves families in two counties and helps to educate teachers in eight school districts. We also hold an annual conference that draws people from all over the state! To think of all the people that this one group has helped is mind-boggling!

It is because of the devotion or sacrifice of individuals that causes become of value. –Julian Huxley

When you want to make things happen, get some people together who feel the same way that you do. Pool your talents, energies, and resources. And watch how quickly it all falls into place. Together in community: Anything is possible; everything is possible!

Real joy comes not from ease or riches or from the praise of men, but from doing something worthwhile.
–Sir Wilfred Grenfell

Doing something worthwhile is a reward in itself. Giving feels good. Sometimes I hear people say that they're too tired to give, or they don't have the time. Where does this feeling of lack come from? Once you give you feel energized! If you feel you have no time, then give what little time you have and it's that much more valuable of a gift! And you'll find that you have more time to give.

We do not have to save the world; the world is not lost, just confused. We do not have to bring something back to God which never left Him. When we get rid of everything which contradicts Reality, our world will be saved. –Ernest Holmes

Prejudice exists because we perceive the differences in our lives rather than the commonalities. Pollution exists because we're thinking of ourselves and not of future generations. The "good" world exists underneath all of this mess; we've now got to see the "mess" for what it is–a contradiction of reality–and clean it up!

DIRECTIONS FOR WEDNESDAY
Be an active member of your community today. Be a good neighbor. Take your neighbors some tomatoes from your garden or lemons from your tree. Offer to bring in the mail when a neighbor is out of town.

Organize a block party. Help out in your children's classrooms. Join a civic organization like Rotary, Toastmasters, or the Optimists Club. Read your local paper and keep up with local happenings. Talk with community leaders about issues of concern to you. Get involved.

THURSDAY: We are One

Travel can be one of the most rewarding forms of introspection.
–Lawrence Durrell

Most of us are pretty ready to accept that we have a connection with our family; it's genetic, after all. And then we may even be able to feel some connection with our neighbors or the people we work with because those people are in our lives on a regular basis and we get comfortable with them. But what about people from different areas, different cultures? It can seem so abstract to talk about connection with people so distant, so different from us.

That's why travel is such an important part of the spiritual journey. It puts us in contact with people we wouldn't ordinarily meet and gives us the opportunity to feel our commonality as a human family.

We have so much more in common than not. A mother loves her children no matter where you go. A craftsman takes pride in his work. A salesman is friendly whatever he's selling and wherever he's selling it! We may not speak the same language, or wear the same clothes, or bring home the same amount of money, but we all share a common human experience. We all feel the same emotions.

When my son Freddy and I were in India, we spent a lot of time with my friend Janie and her son, Towner. Freddy and Towner have so much in common and they had so much fun experiencing this very exotic country together. One day we visited a Hari Krishna temple near Agra where many of the local people come all the time. While we marveled at the beautiful paintings and colorful displays, the local children were very much intrigued with these two young American boys! Towner had his portable CD player with him and let the kids hear the music through the headphones. The look on their faces was pure amazement!

Freddy and Towner made instant friendships that day with children whose lives could not have been more different from theirs.

A man travels the world in search of what he needs and returns home to find it. –George Moore

Then, when you return home, you realize that the only place you'll find love and peace is right where you are. Wherever you are. No one can give it to you; you've got to see it for yourself.

DIRECTIONS FOR THURSDAY
Pay attention to the Oneness of all creation today. Everywhere on earth we're breathing the same air, moving through the same space, looking at the same sky. Feel your connection with the human family today. Take a "virtual" trip and explore another country via the Internet, or check out some guidebooks at the bookstore or library. Where have you been, where would you like to go, who would you like to switch places with for a day?

FRIDAY: Gratitude

Gratitude is the sign of noble souls. –Aesop

There is so much in our lives that we just take for granted. When we stop to think about it, everything we have is a gift that deserves our appreciation. Every day is a new day, and the sun comes up to greet us. How lucky are we? We have access to the wonders in this world at any moment in time. We are refreshed and renewed by the breath of the wind and cleansed by the gentle rain.

Gratitude is the memory of the heart. –Jean Baptiste Massieu

Gratitude is felt in the heart. It's that feeling that warms your heart, where you feel your chest expand and the love permeates every cell of your body. It can be a very healing experience, so allow yourself to feel gratitude several times a day.

A grateful thought toward heaven is of itself a prayer.
–Doris Lessing

If there's just one prayer that's all-purpose, no matter what occasion, it has to be "Thank You." The world is here for us, and we are here for each other.

He enjoys much who is thankful for little; a grateful mind is both a great and a happy mind. –Secker

There is as much greatness of mind in acknowledging a good turn, as in doing it. –Seneca

I don't think it's a coincidence that "grateful" and "greatness" are such similar words. Gratitude gives us peace of mind. It is humbling and solemn. It makes us feel great; it makes us feel the greatness that is already within us!

There shall be
Eternal summer in the grateful heart. –Celia Thaxter

DIRECTIONS FOR FRIDAY
Be grateful today. Give thanks today. Start with making a list of all the things you are grateful for. Say a prayer of thanks. Sing a song of thanks. Chant it, hum it, shout it out! Thank God for all that we have and all that we are. Thank God all day today!

SATURDAY: Time Alone

Let there be space in your togetherness. –Kahlil Gibran

Time alone is a gift we give ourselves that helps us to get there. As much as there is to discover in the outside world, there is all that and more for us to discover in our inner world, our spiritual world. It is when we are alone that we can really feel our connection with God.

Respect the child. Wait and see the new product of Nature.
Be not too much his parent. Trespass not on his solitude.
–Ralph Waldo Emerson

If you are a parent, it's a good idea to get your kids in the habit of spending quiet time alone, just to think or relax. A child will learn the importance of solitude and carry it into his adult life. There would be a lot fewer stressed-out people in this world if all of our parents did this!

Solitude is as needful to the imagination as society is wholesome for the character. –James Russell Lowell

Great ideas come from solitude. I'm sure Einstein spent time alone pondering the universe. Composers work long hours alone, in quiet, in order to "hear" the music. Then they go to the instruments to work out the details. Solitude is an important part of the creative process.

One of the greatest necessities in America is to discover creative solitude. –Carl Sandburg

We have access to all the intelligence of the universe; we have only to quiet our minds to receive it. The ideas are out there all the time, but we can only "get" them, or pay attention to them, when we're quiet.

If we have listening ears, God speaks to us in our own language, whatever that language be. –Mahatma Gandhi

When we're quiet, we can listen. When we listen, we can hear God. God speaks to us, not only with words and sentences that we have pieced together in our minds, but also with music, with beauty, with nature, with love. God's message may be subtle or strong; we just have to listen and not tune it out with the "noise" of our everyday lives.

While we converse with what is above us, we do not grow old, we grow young. –Ralph Waldo Emerson

Time alone, especially time spent in meditation, heals us. It heals our bodies and our spirits, which are intricately connected. Know that this connection takes place within us and use time alone to take care of yourself: body, mind, and spirit.

I have never found the companion that was so companionable as solitude. –Henry David Thoreau
Some people feel awkward going to a movie alone or eating in a restaurant alone. But time alone, even out in public, is good for us! You can really be good company for yourself. Spending time alone you learn that you truly are your own best friend.

Leisure is the most challenging responsibility a man can be offered. –Dr. William Russell

Many of us don't know what to do when we have free time. We're lost. Think of all those retirees who fall into depression just when they thought they'd begin living it up. They don't know what to do with themselves when they're not on a schedule. It's a rare and precious thing, time alone at leisure. Learn what it is you like to do when you're alone.

Only the person who loves himself can enjoy the gift of leisure.
–Henry Gerber

Treat yourself and do what you love to do. And also do nothing! We feel our connection with God in both cases.

I never lose sight of the fact that just being is fun.
–Katherine Hepburn

DIRECTIONS FOR SATURDAY
We can get there by just being. Just being is fun and interesting, and, ultimately, it can be enlightening.

Spend the day all by yourself today. Keep yourself company. Court yourself. Be comfortable with yourself. Talk to yourself. Take yourself out to eat if you feel like it. Do whatever it is that you want to do, but do it alone, without being lonely. Enjoy sweet solitude.

This week was all about connections. We make connections and feel our connections through giving of our time and talents, by spending time together, and by being of service to one another. We reach out to the community of which we are a part because we know that we are all one. We express gratitude for our many gifts on a regular basis and spend time alone to quiet our minds. And with that quiet mind, we can continue our journey into week eight.

Week Eight

Are We There Yet?

KEYWORD: MIND

By now we understand just how powerful we can be in effecting change in our lives. And it all starts from a seed of an idea in our minds. We make a decision, have an intention, make choices to support that intention, and create what it is that we want for ourselves. So, all we have to do is to plant the seeds that we want to grow! Apples come from apple seeds right? Well, success comes from success seeds, not from seeds of doubt or fear. Watch what you put into your mind, because that is what will surely take root!

SUNDAY: Know Yourself

There's only one corner of the universe you can be certain of improving, and that is your own self. –Aldous Huxley

There's no getting there without knowing ourselves. You may wonder why we've waited until Week 8 to deal with something so fundamental. It's because there's so much to us! We are all the things that we've talked about already: nature, love, diversity, timelessness, beauty . . . all of it! We are whole and complete, and yet at the same time we are a part of the greater whole. We are spirit expressed as each of us individually, and we are connected to each other and to God. When we better understand these aspects of ourselves, we can better know ourselves.

We can work diligently at improving our world, but the best way we can do that is to work on ourselves. It all starts right here.

When you try to understand everything, you will not understand anything. The best way is to understand yourself, and then you will understand everything. –Shunryu Suzuki

By better knowing ourselves, by studying ourselves, we are better able to understand the world, since we are each a microcosm of it, a holographic piece of the larger whole.

DIRECTIONS FOR SUNDAY
Know who you are today. Make a list of the roles that you play, the hats that you wear. You do those things, and do them quite wonderfully, but you are not those things. You simply are. Make another list of all the qualities you would associate with God: love, joy, kindness . . .; use words that come to your mind and write them down. You are that. You are love. You are joy. You are kindness. You are Yourself. Think about what that means today and carry it with you.

MONDAY: Education

If you want the present to be different than the past, study the past. –Baruch Spinoza

One key way we can enrich ourselves spiritually is to drink in the knowledge of the universe. We want to learn as much as we can about the world and how it works.

Education is much more than books. It's also learning about each other. The more we learn about each other, the more we come to accept and understand one another. War comes as a result of magnified differences. Peace is the result of trust and understanding.

The secret of education is respecting the pupil.
–Ralph Waldo Emerson

We each may learn in our own way, and sometimes it's difficult to fig-
ure out just which way that is, but our minds can take in and process a
great deal of information. Helen Keller was blind and deaf, yet her
teacher, Annie Sullivan, had the patience and perseverance to find her
student's learning style. Then Helen, this girl that the world had seem-
ingly given up on, went on to teach and inspire so many others. We're
all equally capable of learning.

One of the best ways to stay connected to the learning process is to
read, read, read. I'll always remember going to the library as a little girl
with my mother. I loved to read biographies. I think the stories
appealed to me because they're real! Going to the library instilled in me
a lifelong love of reading. Reading keeps our minds and hearts open to
the world around us.

All of life is our school, every day, everywhere. From a spiritual perspective, we're not really learning as much as we are remembering what
we already know to be true.

Our educations are only of value to us if we actually use them to better ourselves. There's no way we can learn too much. Education can be
a powerful tool. We need to apply what we learn to help others and to
create the world we want to live in.

*We learn from experience. A man never wakes up his second
baby just to see it smile.* –Grace Williams

DIRECTIONS FOR MONDAY
Learn something new today. Or learn several new things. Read. Surf the
Internet. Interview professionals. Start one of those foreign language
classes you've always wanted to take but have put off. Get out a classic
that you've always wanted to read and devour it. Learn from your
experiences. When something happens, is it happening to you? What
can you learn today and every day?

TUESDAY: Knowledge

Intellectually we know that God is Love, but our spiritual
knowledge of God comes through discovering and feeling Him
at the center of our own being. –Ernest Holmes

Education is the learning process. Knowledge is taking what we've
learned and applying it to our lives.

Spiritual lessons are available everywhere, floating around for the taking, even in school. We just have to be open and attuned to them.
Nature is a great teacher. All of our senses pick up the perfection, the
beauty all around us. We can observe the pictures in the clouds or the
two kittens cuddling. We can hear music in the rustle of the autumn
leaves, touch flower petals that feel like velvet, taste the sugary-sour of
lemonade, or smell cinnamon in freshly baked cookies. God is present;
can you sense it?

Nothing becomes real till it is experienced–even a proverb is no
proverb to you till your life has illustrated it. –John Keats

Reading about Paris is obviously not the same thing as going there. We
need to embrace the experiences that come our way and understand
that every experience is an opportunity to learn. Life is a journey, a
process of self-exploration and spiritual growth.

When you know a thing, to hold that you know it, and when you
do not know a thing, to allow that you do not know it: this is
knowledge. –Confucius

Since we've agreed to embark on this journey during our time on earth,
let's approach it like Indiana Jones! Let's be adventurous and explore
everything about ourselves and how we can express ourselves: body,
mind, and spirit. Let's investigate how we create our lives and how we
gain insight from our experiences.

Imagination is more important than knowledge. –Albert Einstein

When we take what we have learned and build on it using our imaginations, wondrous things happen. The inventors, scientists, artists, and educators who think "outside the lines," who dare to break the rules and experiment, have come up with the ideas and plans that have really improved our way of living. Be bold! There are no limits in creative thinking.

DIRECTIONS FOR TUESDAY

What do you know? What are you sure about? Know that God loves you. The world may be many different things to many different people. Understand that it is all in how we perceive ourselves and the world. The truth is, We are One. Take that knowledge and build a foundation of love and faith today.

Let your mind wander today. Explore. Try new things. Go new places. Meet new people. Dream. Think about the possibilities. Have an open mind. Bask in the beauty and the wonder of the world. It is a wonderful world we live in!

WEDNESDAY: Understanding and Curiosity

That is what learning is. You suddenly understand something you've understood your whole life, but in a new way.
–Doris Lessing

Taking in knowledge is such a multi-layered process. There are so many levels of understanding. I've been re-reading some of the books that I read when I was in grade school and middle school because my children are reading them now. I understand so much more now, just being older and more experienced, than I did when I was younger; though I learned from those books then, too. We just have a different perspective as we grow both physically and spiritually, in age and in wisdom. It's like the lightbulb going on over our heads!

In youth we learn, in age we understand.
–Marie Ebner-Eschenbach

This process of learning and learning more and understanding and understanding more goes on all through our lives. I'm sure that if I re-read those books again when my grandchildren go through them, then I will get even more out of them! It's true with just about any material, I think, whether the author intended it to be so or not.

The purpose of learning is growth, and our minds, unlike our bodies, continue growing as we continue to live.
–Mortimer Adler

I've read Shakespeare's *Hamlet* several times now and find it to be one of his most metaphysical plays. I didn't get it the first time around, but I find more and more really incredible messages each time I pick it up. Not because the words have changed any, but because I have grown and changed and can understand them better!

I find the great thing in this world is not so much where we stand, as in what direction we are moving.
–Oliver Wendell Holmes, Sr.

We want to be moving forward; we want to be making progress toward getting there. From wherever we are, if we are moving toward God, following our hearts, then we are going in the right direction.

There's a big difference between knowledge and belief. Belief leaves some room for question. Knowledge is steady and sure. Carl Jung was indeed a knowledgeable man. He had a sign over the front door at his home that read: "Called or not called, God is present."

Wonder rather than doubt is the fruit of knowledge.
–Abraham Joshua Heschel

Learning gets us thinking about possibilities. It's those "what if" questions that can lead to great discoveries.

I do not feel obliged to believe that the same God who has endowed us with sense, reason, and intellect has intended us to forgo their use. –Galileo Galilei

We're given these minds to use. So let's put them to good use!

The last function of reason is to recognize that there are an infinity of things which surpass it. –Blaise Pascal

Some things can't be explained; they're beyond all reason. That's one of the wonders of the world, that there is so much out there beyond our current reasoning and understanding. But that should only make us strive to learn more, to solve these mysteries, and to experience more fully our connection with God.

A mind all logic is like a knife all blade. It makes the hand bleed that uses it. –Rabindranath Tagore

Not everything is logical. We've got to leave space for human compassion and gut instincts. Dr. Paul Pearsall has written a book called *The Heart's Code*, which explains the research he did to prove that the heart literally thinks. Now that does not sound logical, but it is true, and Dr. Pearsall scientifically proved it. This is ground-breaking, magnificent information which opens up to us a wealth of opportunities.

I am not young enough to know everything. –James M. Barrie

Sometimes our best teachers are young children. It's amazing some of the things that kids say without even thinking about it. One weekend when basketball practice was scheduled at the same time as church, I told my son Brian that he would have to miss church that day so that he could attend practice. He told me he would rather go to church. "Really?" I said. He looked me straight in the eye and said, "Don't you think that's more important?" He was right.

Minds are like parachutes: they only function when open. –Thomas Robert Dewar

When our minds are open, we're ready to receive information and gain knowledge. If our minds are closed, we're not going to learn anything. An open mind lends itself to open discussion, to different points of view, to differing opinions, to unlimited possibilities.

*Thoughts are things; therefore every man has the ability within
himself to alter everything that is wrong in his life.*
–Ernest Holmes

Anything that you can think of, you can achieve. If you can picture it,
you can have it. We wouldn't have the thought to change something in
our lives if it were not possible to do so. The process of creation starts
in our minds, with a thought or an idea.

WEDNESDAY: Curiosity

*Curiosity is the only intelligence test which tells what one may
become as well as what one is.* –Saturday Review

Curiosity spurs us on to learn more, to experiment, to search out and
discover. We have more opportunities available to us when we're curious and are willing to look in different places for them.

*The most important thing is to not stop questioning. Curiosity
has its own reason for existing.* –Albert Einstein

Curiosity compels us to learn and to grow. It is our nature to be curious
and we should embrace our curiosity and encourage it in our children.

A blossom must break the sheath it has been sheltered by.
–Phyllis Bottome

We have a certain comfort zone in our lives. We're comfortable with
what we're familiar with. But we can't grow if we just stay put. We've
got to go out and experience in order to bloom.

*The mind of man is capable of anything–because everything is
in it, all the past as well as all the future.* –Joseph Conrad

Because we have access to an unlimited amount of knowledge, there
are no limits on our potential accomplishments. We are truly capable of
anything!

Time ripens all things. No man is born wise.
–Miguel De Cervantes

A combination of knowledge and experience breeds wisdom. Wisdom is a deep knowingness, a mature affirmation of God's presence.

Intuition is the hidden wellspring of life, the avenue through which we get back our lost vision. –Ernest Holmes

Our intuition comes into play when we are tuned in to God. Whether we hear the message or feel it, or see it, we've got to pay attention to it. Our intuition is there to serve us, so make use of it.

DIRECTIONS FOR WEDNESDAY

Be curious today. Check out something you've been meaning to explore. Ask your intuition for guidance. Spend the day consciously keeping your mind wide open to new experiences, new lessons. Try something new, ask questions, seek out answers.

THURSDAY: Wisdom

Get wisdom: and with all thy getting get understanding.
–Proverbs 4:7

Don't get wisdom mixed up with information. We are inundated with a vast amount of information these days; it's information overload in many cases with the Internet, cable and digital television channels, local and national newspapers and magazines. Since we have a choice, look for wisdom first. Turn to the Source.

True wisdom comes from within. So, after we've heard everyone else's opinions and advice, it's best to consult with ourselves! Quiet your mind and find out what that still, small voice inside is telling you. That's God talking! Some people say, "listen to your heart" or "feel it in your gut." It's all the same thing. Biologically, it's your body expressing its innate wisdom. Take heed! It's there for a reason!

Pursue knowledge, learn from experience, pay attention to your intuition. All of these things help us to gain wisdom and a deeper understanding of ourselves and our purpose. All of these things help us to get there.

The price of wisdom is above rubies. –Job 28:18

Wisdom has more value in our lives than any material thing that we could ever want. It takes time to attain wisdom, and it is very precious. Wisdom comes from God, and from knowing our connection with God.

A prudent question is one-half wisdom. –Francis Bacon

There is no dumb question. The wise among us know that we need to ask to get answers. We need to ask for help when we need it and not be afraid to raise our hands! Knowing that answers are out there and help is available to us is a sure step toward wisdom.

DIRECTIONS FOR THURSDAY
Celebrate and honor wisdom today. Think about all the best teachers you've had all through your life, and give thanks for all that those people taught you. Tap into your inner wisdom today. Listen to yourself. Follow your intuition. Feel that "gut instinct." Know that all the wisdom of the world is available to you at any moment. Ask the universe a question and look for its guidance. You'll see the way!

FRIDAY: Honesty

Honesty is the first chapter in the book of wisdom.
–Thomas Jefferson

Our inner guidance is always honest with us. How honest are we with ourselves? How honest are we with each other? To get there, we need to realize that there is no place for anything less than pure integrity and honesty.

No legacy is so rich as honesty. –William Shakespeare

It's such a compliment when we hear someone praised as being honest and fair. It seems so refreshing in these times when marketing and sales tactics have us all fooled into believing outlandish claims! There's a spiritual simplicity with being honest. It's a virtue that is universally recognized as admirable.

When we really live truth, we will cease to talk about it.
–Elbert Hubbard

Tell the Truth. It's that simple. To be honest is to be wise. Be honest with yourself and with everyone you come into contact with. Don't lie, cheat, or steal. Live honestly; it's the smart thing to do.

DIRECTIONS FOR FRIDAY
Be honest today. Don't lie. Don't exaggerate. Be real. Be truthful. This doesn't mean that you don't have respect, manners, and tact. It means that you are honest with yourself and that you do the right thing because you know the right thing to do.

SATURDAY: Teaching

To teach is to learn. –Japanese proverb

One way to express spirit in the world is to teach what we know. Actually, if you think about it, we're always teaching, just like we are always learning.

The art of teaching is the art of assisting discovery.
–Mark Van Doren

Which teachers have made an impression on your life? I can think of many that I've had who are still important to me today–not just because of what they taught me, but how they made me feel about myself. Mrs. Eaton in the first grade made me feel smart. She appreciated my enthusiasm for learning and always encouraged me to do more than was expected. My fifth-grade teacher, Miss McCall, loved to travel, and she brought stories from all over the world into our classroom, which fascinated me and stimulated my curiosity. In college, I had a screenwriting professor who gave me the best advice I've ever received about writing. He said, "Don't get it right, get it written!" Thanks to him, I've been able to get words actually onto the page without stressing about making them perfect.

I appreciate so much the teachers who have made a difference in my children's lives. Helene Koperberg had my son Freddy for three years of elementary school, and her genuine love and concern for her students made school a very successful experience for him. Jon Andreas, who taught my son Brian in the sixth grade, emphasized character and values with his students and stimulated their love of history by bringing in examples from *Star Wars!*

I am grateful that I have often had the opportunity to teach both adults and children. Teaching is so rewarding, and I always feel so good and energized after class!

DIRECTIONS FOR SATURDAY
Be a student and a teacher today. When we teach, we learn. What can you teach that would be of value to someone? Give of your talents and knowledge by teaching. Help someone to learn something. There are many opportunities for involvement. Check your local library, for they often need volunteers for adult literacy classes. A bookstore in our area holds Monday night chess classes, and more experienced players teach beginners how to play. You might teach camp songs to a Girl Scout troop or teach a child to tie his shoe. Teach today, and see how much you learn.

This week we focused on our MIND. We got to know ourselves and who we really are. We broadened our horizons by pursuing education and developing our knowledge and understanding. We know how important it is to explore and to be curious and at the same time pay attention to our inner wisdom. We understand the value of honesty and the true rewards of teaching.

It's been eight weeks, and we've come really far! But don't stop now . . . there's still more to do, and do it we shall, as we learn to take ACTION!

Week Nine

The Welcome Wagon

KEYWORD: ACTION

This is Week Nine, and we traveled a long way to get here. This week is about taking what we've learned and applying it in our lives for the maximum benefit. We've got to walk our talk! It's time to take action!

SUNDAY: Doing the Best We Can Do

When we do the best we can, we never know what miracle is wrought in our life, or in the life of another. –Helen Keller

We accumulate all this knowledge, and learn so much every day, yet it is all meaningless if we don't apply it in our lives. We apply it by taking action, by doing. We can't get there with our eyes shut. We've got to be aware and awake and active. We've got to consciously work toward our goals to achieve them. Doing, taking action–these are the keys to living in spirit.

There is a vast difference between knowing what to do and doing what we know. –Ernest Holmes

At this point, we should know what to do to get there. Now we just have to do it! We need to connect what we know with what we do and then the "getting there" will seem to come to us.

Skill to do comes of doing. –Ralph Waldo Emerson

It's as if we're at the gate, just waiting for permission to take off! We don't need anyone's permission but our own! The time to start is now. The place to begin is here. It may seem like you have to remind yourself just exactly where you are going for a while. But then, eventually, practicing these lessons, embodying these skills, will all become as natural as they are meant to be. Just keep taking action, and you'll soon be a skilled action-taker!

I hear and I forget. I see and I remember. I do and I understand.
–Chinese proverb

Lots of people have ideas, but few actually act on them! When you have an idea, make a plan of action and strive every day toward turning your dream into a reality. How much time we spend on an idea shows how committed we are to it.

God must eternally express His Intelligence by eternally doing something–eternally acting. Hence the necessity of human achievement. It is inevitable and has behind it a Divine urge.
–Ernest Holmes

We are creators and are driven to create. We are always doing something, even when we're doing nothing. Don't get me wrong. Doing nothing sometimes is great. It's especially good when we're connecting with God. Take a look at what else you're doing and how you spend your time. Could it be put to better use?

DIRECTIONS FOR SUNDAY
Be aware of what you are doing today. How are you spending your time? What tasks are you giving priority? How can you change your daily routine to reflect your goal of getting there? Use what you know. Take action today. Work on yourself inside and outside, personally, professionally, and globally.

MONDAY:Multi-Sensory

Moral qualities rule the world, but at short distances, the senses are despotic. –Ralph Waldo Emerson

Getting there involves working with all our senses: taste, smell, touch, hearing, sight. Our senses are our connection to the physical plane. They can help us to be present, to live in the now. They can evoke memories, stimulate our imaginations, and carry us off to distant lands. Our senses are part of what's really fun about being human! Let's use them to their fullest advantage and appreciate all that they can do for us.

There is in souls a sympathy with sounds, and as the wind is pitched the ear is pleased with melting airs or martial, brisk or grave; some chord in unison with what we hear is touched within us, and the heart replies. –William Cowper

We've already talked about how wonderful music can be, but there are sounds in nature which can be even more beautiful to hear: the ocean, a bird singing, a baby's contented coo. Pay attention to what is going on sound-wise all around you, and strive for harmony.

Nothing awakens a reminiscence like an odor. –Victor Hugo

It doesn't take much to bring up a memory when an odor is involved. Think of certain smells that bring up fond events in your life: newly mown grass, cinnamon sticks, fresh-cut lemons. Aromatherapy is a popular science right now, and it works really well, too!

Touch is the landscape
of what is possible. –Kate Green

Babies get comfort from their familiar blankets. It's the touch, the contact with the skin, that makes them feel secure. How does it feel to hold the hand of a loved one? Feel the rich texture of a cashmere sweater. Let sand run through your fingers.

A truly elegant taste is generally accompanied with excellency of heart. –Henry Fielding

When people talk about "good taste" they generally mean an appreciation for quality or style. But this most likely came from the taste that we experience on our tongues! It's discretionary; everyone experiences taste differently. Experiment a little with taste: sweet, sour, salty, bitter, pungent, astringent. Appreciate food for its diversity of tastes. Try something new, something exotic!

What delights us in visible beauty is the invisible.
–Marie von Ebner-Eschenbach

Our gift of sight allows us to experience all things beautiful, and there are so many beautiful things to see! What we begin to realize, when we are getting there, is what makes these things beautiful is what we can't see with our human eyes, and that is spirit.

DIRECTIONS FOR MONDAY

Pay attention to your senses today. Breathe in and smell the sweet morning air. Stroke your cat and feel his soft fur and the vibration of his welcoming purr. Listen to beautiful music, the sounds of children laughing, or the wind through the trees. Really taste your meals today. Connect how the food looks and smells with how it tastes and feel the textures on your tongue. See the beauty of God all around you. Listen to your inner voice, your intuition, when making choices today. Be awake, be aware.

TUESDAY: In Practice, Not Just Theory

One man practicing sportsmanship is far better than fifty preaching it. –Knute K. Rockne

I don't know where it originated, but we all know the expression "actions speak louder than words." It's true in every aspect of life. Live the example. Do what needs to be done.

Are we walking our talk? Are we taking our own advice? It's one thing to know what the right thing to do is; it's another thing to actually do it. If we really mean it, if we really care, then we'll act on our convictions.

As I grow older I pay less attention to what men say. I just watch what they do. –Andrew Carnegie

Part of living an honest life is aligning our words and our actions. If you make a promise, keep it. If you say you'll do something, do it.

DIRECTIONS FOR TUESDAY

Watch your behavior today. Behave now the way you truly want to be when you get there. You're closer than you think.

WEDNESDAY: Attitude

Happiness is not a state to arrive at, but a manner of traveling.
–Margaret Lee Runbeck

Just as we can choose an attitude of optimism, we can choose an attitude of happiness. We might as well be happy getting there. It's a big spiritual lesson to know that happiness is a choice. You've got a choice, so why not choose to be happy?!

A willing heart adds feather to the heel. –Joanna Baillie

Our attitude is reflected in our work. If we love what we do, it shows, and everyone knows it. And when we have enthusiasm for our work, it makes work a joy for us!

Enthusiasm raises the artist above himself . . . in an ordinary mood one would not have been able to accomplish many of the things for which enthusiasm lends one everything, energy, fire.
–Clara Schumann

We can go a long way on this journey with a little enthusiasm. Enthusiasm is contagious, and you can end up bringing a lot of people along with you!

DIRECTIONS FOR WEDNESDAY

Remember that attitude is our choice. Always. Choose to have a good attitude today. Don't let things get you down. Be optimistic, be positive, be enthusiastic. Smile. Be happy. Love your life, love yourself.

THURSDAY: The Past is the Passed

Nothing is so soothing to our self-esteem as to see our bad traits in our forebears. It seems to absolve us. –Van Wyck Brooks

We might want to blame our bad behaviors on our ancestors by saying, "it's in the genes." But that's no excuse. We are living now and making choices today. We can take action to change our behaviors and change our lives.

If you cannot get rid of the family skeleton, at least make it dance. –George Bernard Shaw

We may not be able to change the past, but we sure can learn from it. We can bring the old skeletons into the light and turn them into something positive.

A wise man will make haste to forgive, because he knows the full value of time and will not suffer it to pass away in unnecessary pain. –Rambler

Forgive, forgive, forgive. Don't hang on to old hurts; let go . . . free yourself from that burden! Grudges are heavy and hard to carry. Lighten your load!

DIRECTIONS FOR THURSDAY
Release the past today. Realize that every day is a new day and that you can be a new person. Forgive others who have hurt you in the past. Forgive yourself for whatever you may feel you have done wrong in the past. Understand that the past is over and that forgiveness is healing. Release the old with love, let it go. Take a deep breath and blow it away. Feel better.

FRIDAY: Stepping into the Future

The Future . . . something which everyone reaches at the rate of sixty minutes an hour, whatever he does, whoever he is. –C. S. Lewis

We know that there is always a future and that there is always something to look forward to. Time keeps marching on. There will always be more to see and more to do. There will always be more room to grow.

The best preparation for the future, is the present well seen to, and the last duty done." –G. Macdonald

Everything that we're doing right now is preparing us for the future. We're making ourselves better people and, in turn, the world a better place.

If there were no future life, our souls would not thirst for it. –Johann Paul Friedrich Richter

Part of being human is having that "thirst" or ambition to improve our lives. This is a good thing. We can learn a lot because of this.

DIRECTIONS FOR FRIDAY
Look optimistically toward a bright future today. Do not live in the future, but know that the future holds good things for you. Go ahead with plans with confidence. Act now to make your dreams a reality.

SATURDAY: Live Now!

Since Time is not a person we can overtake when he is gone, let us honor him with mirth and cheerfulness of heart while he is passing. –Johann Wolfgang von Goethe

Living in the moment, being aware of the present, living NOW, is probably the most important lesson we have to learn. When we can do this, we can get there without any effort at all, because we will realize where we are supposed to be. We will understand that "here" *is* "there!" You know those directories you see in a shopping mall or a large office building? As a point of reference, they will say, "You are here." Look at the truth in that simple statement! Wherever you go, even when you get "there," you are "here." Enjoy this space you're in and be fully present in it.

*Try to be happy in this very present moment; and put not off
being so to a time to come; as though that time should be of
another make from this, which is already come, and is ours.*
–Buckminster Fuller

Why wait for happiness? Why postpone delight? Do you think you
have to earn it? This is our divine right! We are as happy as we decide
to be. We make our own choices and we can choose to accept and recognize the bliss that is already ours.

*Look upon every day as the whole of life, not merely as a section;
and enjoy and improve the present without wishing, through
haste, to rush on to another.* –Johann Paul Friedrich Richter

I saw a great watch the other day that is a wonderful reminder about
time. It had a big ONE written across the face, and in smaller letters, it
spelled out Only Now Exists!

DIRECTIONS FOR SATURDAY
It's been said that the past is history, the future's a mystery, but the
present is a gift, and that is why it is called the present. Look at where
you are today. Look at how far you've come. Live this day as you wish
to live all the days of your life, with love.

*Life loves to be taken by the label and told, "I'm with you kid.
Let's go."* –Maya Angelou

Let's approach this journey boldly. Let's go!

Congratulations on completing this nine-week journey! We've come a
long way and covered a lot of ground. You know what you need to do,
and you know that it's up to you. Go for it!

Every day is a new day, full of new opportunities and new choices.
Every day, you're a new person, having changed and grown from the
experiences that you've already gone through to get you to this point.
New day, new you. How far can you get? Maybe today's the day you'll
get there!

Addendum

The Map

There are no new truths, but only truths that have not been recognized by those who have perceived them without noticing. A truth is something that everyone can be shown to know and to have known as people say, all along. –Mary McCarthy

My life is my message. –Mahatma Gandhi

Take all the keywords from the nine-week course and string them together. This is the Truth, this is how to get there:

LOVE ALL CREATION.

LIVE NOW RESPONSIBLY.

CONNECT MIND & ACTION.

That's it! So, get going. . . . I'll meet you there!